"Never Forget"

REQUIEM

REQUIEM
IMAGES OF GROUND ZERO

Photography and Text by
GARY MARLON SUSON

FDNY Honorary Battalion Chief
Official Photographer at Ground Zero for the Uniformed Firefighters Association

Forewords by FDNY Deputy Assistant Chief of
Operations Joseph W. Pfeifer and FDNY Battalion
Chief William C. Hines

BARNES
& NOBLE
BOOKS
NEW YORK

ISBN 978-0-7607-3811-5

Designer: Lynne Yeamans
Photography Editor: Christopher Bain

Color separations by Professional Graphics Inc.
Printed in England by Butler Tanner and Dennis Ltd.

3 5 7 9 10 8 6 4
Third Edition 2010

FRONT ENDPAPERS: Spring 2002. The respect that firefighters have for a fallen brother is clearly shown in the body language of these men during an early morning Honor Guard ceremony on the exit ramp.

BACK ENDPAPERS: Late at night, a volunteer chaplain says a prayer into the handy talky receiver over the body of a fallen firefighter in March 2002.

ABOVE: January 2002. A message of remembrance scrawled on a destroyed fire truck at Ground Zero.

PAGE 1: A worn and cracked leather helmet represents a career spent in the art of rescue.

PAGE 2: "Old Glory Stands Strong." Sunset at Ground Zero. Sunday, September 16, 2001.

DEDICATION

This book is dedicated to my mother, Sherry Suson, and my father, Morry Suson, for noticing that I had an artistic eye at age twelve and putting a camera in my hands. Had you not pushed me to develop my craft, this book would not exist. Thank you both for being so persistent and believing in my abilities.

I also dedicate this book in loving memory to the thousands of innocent civilians, firefighters, police officers, E.M.S. workers, airline employees, airline passengers, and governmental employees who simply went to work on the morning of September 11, 2001. I regret that there are more than three thousand of you that I will never have the chance to meet. May your memories live on forever through your loved ones. Hopefully, through these images, the world will never forget you.

Lastly, I dedicate this 3rd edition, 2010 reprint to Firefighter Rudy Sanfilippo, formerly the Manhattan Trustee of the Uniformed Firefighters Association. Rudy, thanks for placing trust in me to capture such important history; to portray the compassion in which the recovery workers did their job, to put a face on the victims and to give 9/11 families a photographic record of the circumstances surrounding the attempted rescue efforts and recovery of their loved ones.

Special Thanks to Daniel A. Nigro

"The bald eagle, upon seeing a large storm, will shriek with delight, as he knows that the updraft in that storm will take him to heights higher than he has ever reached."
—*Anonymous*

"TIME has a way of dulling our memory and people may forget what happened and the valuable lives lost on 9/11. I hope my images will insure that people never forget."
—*Gary Marlon Suson, BBC Radio 2002*

GOD BLESS AMERICA
LAND OF THE FREE AND HOME OF THE BRAVE

———

More photographs may be viewed online at

WWW.GROUNDZEROMUSEUM.COM
&
WWW.SEPTEMBERELEVEN.NET

———

SPECIAL THANKS

Fire Department of New York, Port Authority Police Department, New York City Police Department, Sharon Suson, Morry Suson, United States Navy, John Vigiano & Family, Beth Ann Morean, Wendy & Bill LaTorre, Andrej Hlinka, Rudy Sanfilippo, Daniel Nigro, Mitties DeChamplain, In Memory of Ron DeChamplain, Omayra Rivera, St. Paul's Chapel, Christopher Keenan, Christy Ferer, In Memory of Neil Levin, Valeria Menapace, Edward Persaud, Mercedes Robles, Melissa Albers, Angela J. Sakaris, Chelsea D'Aprile, Annie Chang, In Memory of Dr. Thomas Stone, Michael Bellone, Al Manigault, Dr. Douglas Cook & Staff in Suring, Wisconsin, "TEAM DEPOT", Home Depot, Joe Miccoli, Steven E. Suson, Jodi Lynn Suson, Marie Pizano, Jeremy Snell, Daren Booth, DELTA Airlines, Arnold Roma, Butler Tanner & Dennis Printing UK, Bobby Anzalone, Jim Doyle, Richard Vander Heyden, Qihang Cai, The Spanier Family, John Esty, Globe Lithographing Co., Arthur Stanton, Bob Lion, Jeff Hirsch & FOTOCARE, *The New York Times*, The Geidel Family, Bob Busch, Stephen Zaderiko, Joe Pfeifer, George Pataki, Clarus Corp., The Citizens of the Great Country of Italy, Lee Ielpi, Jim Riches, Annette Uptain, Hans Paessler, James Gladstone, Barrington High School, Tracy Chow, Ron Spadafora, Edgar A. Domenech, Dr. Douglas King, Luis Rivera, Dr. Michael Smatt, FAUS Corporation, Jan Ramirez, Stephen Reisig, American Airlines, United Airlines, Nicholas Scoppetta, Richard M. Daley, N.Y.C. Department of Sanitation, In Memory of Dee Guskind, The Uptain Family, Jack Mooney, George Riley, Federal Bureau of Investigation, The Downey Family, United States Army, United States Air Force, United States Marines, Neil Poch & Tour Mate Systems in Canada, Edith Chapin, *CNN*, David Asman, George Rush, Jack Tipping & Family, Paula Zahn, *SKY* News, MAMIYA Camera Corp., Carhartt Corp., *The Bergen Record*, Ground Zero Ironworkers, Dennis O'Berg & Family, Bill Butler, E.M.S. Workers, University of Texas at Austin, U.S. Coast Guard, In Memory of Tim Moore, Susan Sachs, The Generous Citizens of England, Tom Cruise, Carmen Hippke, Henry Kissane, Salvatore Cassano, In Memory of Tommy Wonder, Peter Hayden, *N.Y. Daily News, The Associated Press*, Robert DeNiro, Ken Feinberg, Todd Lefkovic, Dave Levin, Arissona Negron, George Hubbard, Ed Sweeney & Family, The Surviving Families of the Victims of September 11 and In Memory of Anne Frank.

FOREWORD

Deputy Assistant Chief of Operations Joseph W. Pfeifer

September 11 began for me in the firehouse kitchen. The night tour was ending and the firefighters for the day shift were just coming in with bagels and rolls for breakfast. At around 8:30 A.M., the firefighter on housewatch received an alarm and announced over the loudspeaker system in the firehouse, *"E. 7, L.1, and Battalion 1, everyone goes for an odor of natural gas at the corner of Church Street and Lispenard Street."* It was a beautiful, clear day as the fire apparatus, sirens blasting, headed to the emergency. We were about a dozen blocks north of the World Trade Center; it was in our direct line of sight. After some checking around we found a slight gas odor in the street. This was just a normal, routine emergency. At 8:46 A.M. there would be nothing normal or routine anymore. We heard the unusual sound of a commercial plane flying low overhead. The jet roared past us and headed south. Within seconds we saw the plane aim for the World Trade Center and crash into the upper floors of the North Tower. There was a huge fireball, then a couple of seconds later we heard the explosion.

My heart was racing as a thousand things went through my mind. I knew that I was a chief at what would be one of the biggest fires in the history of New York City. I immediately transmitted a second alarm, followed shortly by a third alarm with specific tactical orders. In the lobby of the North Tower, ninety floors from where the plane impacted the building, there were severely injured people and extensive damage. Within minutes a number of higher-ranking fire chiefs gathered and we decided on a rescue plan to save thousands of people who were trapped or needed assistance. As the firefighters came into the lobby we gave them the order to ascend the stairs to implement the different aspects of the rescue plan. One lieutenant from Engine 33 came over to me and without saying a word waited for orders. I told him that the early reports put the fire around the 78th floor and not to go any higher than the 70th floor, where we could coordinate the rescue of those trapped above. Then, as if time stood still, we remained motionless, staring at each other, concerned if the other would be okay. The lieutenant turned around, gathered his men, and walked to the stairs to start the rescue. That was the last time I saw my brother Kevin.

At 9:58 A.M. the South Tower collapsed and the lobby of the North Tower went totally dark from the debris. In the darkness, unaware what exactly had taken place, I pressed the button on my portable radio and transmitted to the firefighters, *"Command to all units in Tower One, EVACUATE the building...."* We slowly escaped to the street and started to regroup near the front of the North Tower when suddenly the Tower started to collapse. Again the area went totally black but this time it was outside in the street. After the loud roar of the collapsing building, there was complete silence and darkness. After a few seconds of wondering if I was still alive I got up and walked back toward what was the World Trade Center to view this incomprehensible pile of twisted steel and fire.

Every day and every night for months, firefighters and rescue workers searched the pile. First, the hope was to find someone alive, and then the hope was to recover the body of a loved one. The photographs in this book show that struggle. On the face of every firefighter are the pain and determination to find the 2,823 lost loved ones. And in the eyes of these firefighters and rescue workers is the agony that the person they find might be one of their own. These emotions are so strong, so powerful, so personal that only the lens of a photographer who has immersed himself in the world of the firefighters could capture them. Gary Suson is one of those rare photographers. For ten months Gary entered the esoteric world of the firefighters and rescuers of Ground Zero. Through his photographs you get a glimpse of Ground Zero the way the firefighters saw it. And you get the unique perspective of seeing the firefighters labor through the aftermath of the attack.

On Sunday, February 3, 2002, my brother Kevin was recovered. With members from Engine 33, we carried him out on a stretcher draped in an American flag. It was about 7:30 at night and Ground Zero was dark except for the floodlights. I remember carrying him through the field of twisted steel and construction cranes. Each step was overwhelming as I realized the magnitude of what had happened. This was my fire, my building, my people, my firefighters, my brother. We walked up a dirt hill where more than one hundred firefighters and rescue workers saluted.

About a month later, I was working in the First Division in Lower Manhattan when I received a phone call from Battalion Chief Bill Hines. He told me that Gary Suson, a photographer, had some photographs and wanted to meet me. The photograph he had for me was the exact picture I described above. Gary captured not only the scene of the salute as we walked up the dirt hill but the emotions of the moment. As you look closely at Gary's book you see a photo of a firefighter clinging to an American flag and to the memories of a lost brother. It is a picture not of despair, but of extreme pride that the heroes of 9/11 saved thousands and preserved the right of freedom for all people.

Throughout this book Gary captures not only the events of Ground Zero but also the personal emotions of that moment. September 11 is a part of history that we should never forget. Writers record events so we can remember what took place. But it is a photographer like Gary, along with his photos, who allows us to remember the feelings of Ground Zero. Firefighters pictured at the World Trade Center are now the national symbol of what it means to be a hero. My definition of a hero is one who does the ordinary right thing at an extraordinary time. I see those firefighters, and all those who lost their lives trying to help others in ordinary ways at this extraordinary world event, as the real heroes.

—Deputy Assistant Chief of Operations Joseph W. Pfeifer
Fire Department of New York

FOREWORD

Battalion Chief William C. Hines

September 11, 2001, still seems unreal to me at times. It was a day of fate; horrible fate. Too many good people and good friends lost their lives that day. If it had been twenty-four hours earlier or later, 344* different firefighters would have met their fate. I know this because firefighters are all the same. We do our job. We're proud of what we do. People depend on us. If you know anything about firefighters—in fact, any emergency worker—nothing is going to stand in the way of us carrying out our task.

I work in Battalion 7 of the New York City Fire Department, which is located in the Chelsea section of Manhattan. My shift was not scheduled to work on 9/11. I was at home when I awoke to a phone call from a friend and firefighter who was also off that day. He told me that a plane, maybe a tourist plane, had just struck one of the Twin Towers. I remember turning on the television, seeing the North Tower burning, and saying, "It looks like a tough one. The guys are going to take a beating." Just then, the second plane hit. At first I

thought it was a replay of the first plane hitting. But then reality hit me like a punch in the stomach. Both my buddy and I said, "I'll see you down there. Be safe." I think we said it at the same time. Nothing else had to be said. Five seconds after I hung up the phone, it rang again. It was my brother, who is an NYPD Captain. He was in a car responding to the Towers. He immediately professed the thought of terrorism. I told him to be careful and started out of the house. I stopped at both my children's schools to make sure they were taken care of. I then called my wife, who is a teacher, and told her that I'd fill her in at some point. Little did I know that that would be a day and a half later.

The terrorist attack of 9/11/01 is said to be the most documented event in American history. This is important, as we cannot and will not ever forget this malicious and cowardly act of war against innocent people, an act that has been documented so future generations can see that hate and harm to fellow men cannot be tolerated. But there is another side to this event that has not been recorded to the same extent as the tragedy itself. This is the truly inspiring account of the rescue and recovery process that followed. There were many great acts of courage that were performed during the operation. After the Towers came down, there were heroic acts taking place throughout the affected area, not only at the World Trade Center site, but also in the surrounding buildings. Firefighters, police officers, EMS workers, crane operators, and ironworkers all swarmed the site. Every one of these people who responded represents what this country is all about. Everyone involved worked side by side amidst the fires, twisted steel, and rubble with one goal in mind: to rescue as many people as possible. As time passed, the intensity and passion to recover as many victims as possible was just as strong as it was on day one. I consider it an honor and a privilege to have worked with all of the people who were involved with the rescue and recovery effort. My fellow firefighters are the best at what they do. They are second to none. The NYPD, PAPD, EMS, and FEMA USAR team workers were the definition of dedication and professionalism. To the Red Cross, Salvation Army, and other volunteers who supplied us with everything from food and tools to Band-Aids and toothbrushes: thank you. And last, but certainly not least, I want to acknowledge all of the crane operators and ironworkers who made it possible for us to move the twisted steel remains in order for us to carry out our searches. We could not have done our job without you.

In the pages that follow, you will see the work of Gary Suson, a freelance photographer who I met in January 2002 during the recovery process. I was moved by the man's devotion and dedication to capturing the recovery effort going on at the WTC site. What really impressed me about Mr. Suson was his genuine concern for what the workers were experiencing, both physically and emotionally. He thought that his photos could help some in the grieving and healing process. He regularly sought out workers and offered them photos of their efforts. Through the course of the recovery, Mr. Suson compiled a collection of photos that has captured the very spirit of every worker who put time in at the WTC site. Nowhere else have I seen a collection like this dedicated to the recovery efforts.

As I look at his photos, I find myself racing through a range of emotions. Mr. Suson has captured the feelings that many of us have experienced since September 11. Not only are the photos truly inspiring, but they are professionally and tastefully done. This is a collection that is just as important to share as the images of that fateful day. His collection will serve as an important document of the extraordinary recovery efforts and the people who carried them out. It will also play a vital role in the continuing healing process for many people. Thank you, Mr. Suson, for your labor of love.

—*Battalion Chief William C. Hines*
Battalion 7, Fire Department of New York

*Reflects the total number of members lost from FDNY and Fire Patrol.

INTRODUCTION

My fingers were beginning to go numb through my cotton gloves and I set my camera bag down to search one of my many overall pockets for my hand warmers, a valuable commodity in this little world called Ground Zero. The winds were whipping down into the south pit on this arctic February morning at 4:00 A.M. I ripped the hand warmers open, shook them, and stuffed them into my gloves. For seven weeks I had been dreading the thought of traveling to this part of the hole, where the first thirty-five or so floors of the South Tower had been compressed like an accordion to twenty-five feet (8m), but I knew I had to come here eventually. Job application forms, blue office carpet, and red fire alarm boxes stuck out of the twisted rebar wire that once reinforced the structure of each floor. It resembled the layers of a California Redwood tree—layers of an era, layers of humanity—now reduced to crosscut sections of only 11 inches (28cm) per floor. Inside were trapped souls that wanted to go home. My cell phone rang. It was my friend calling from a trendy nightclub. "Gary, where did you go?" He thought I needed a break from my duties as archive photographer for the Uniformed Firefighters Association at Ground Zero. He was concerned that I wasn't taking a break and thought I needed to go out and unwind.

Two hours earlier I had been standing at the bar of a trendy nightclub with him and a girlfriend of his. Music blared and everyone seemed not to have a care in the world. They looked so happy and beautiful, and I felt very out of place. Perhaps I had been in the hole too long? Was I Ground Zeroed out? Maybe my friend was right. "So, you're a photographer? What do you shoot? Like, models?" asked the girl, who knew my friend well. I replied, "Not exactly. I document the recovery at Ground Zero." Looking back, I should have made up some phony career, because all I did was open myself up for more pain. A confused look came over her face as she said, "Oh. Wow. Is that still going on? I thought that was over. Are they still finding people?"

I guess I shouldn't have been surprised by her words because for so many people life had gone on. They had no idea what was going on at Ground Zero, which only served to strengthen my purpose: to expose myself to harsh physical and emotional conditions day in and day out with the goal of telling the photographic story of the recovery. "Yes, I replied," a lump growing in my throat, "It's still going on." "Can I ask you something?" she persisted, leaning in closer. "Sure," I humbly replied. "Have you actually seen people? You know, victims?" this naive young girl said, standing in her Versace pants and shiny halter top. It was like asking an Italian restaurant owner if he had ever seen a pizza. I instantly thought about all my firemen friends back in the hole, digging on their hands and knees at that very moment. I knew exactly where I belonged and it certainly wasn't in this world of cool music and hip people. I leaned into her ear, my stomach turning, and said, "Can I give you some advice? Never ask questions that require answers you may not be able to handle." She looked blankly at me and sipped her drink.

In truth she had done nothing wrong. She was curious, like everyone was, about what it was like down there. The television image of the collapsing Towers looked so much like a special effects movie that many people couldn't connect with the reality of it all. It was more my problem: it was not my time to be out socializing. I was focused on my job and was not prepared for questions of that nature. Dealing with the feelings that those questions brought about would have to come

Gary Suson in the PATH train station under Ground Zero

later, when the recovery was over. Disturbed, I walked away from the bar, out the door, past the black-clad model/doorman, down the stairs, and past the throngs of people waiting to get in.

Back home, the dress pants and sweater came off and on went my Carhartt overalls, boots, sweatshirt, and gas mask. Thirty minutes later I was back where I belonged, doing what I felt compelled to do. I stepped from one extreme into another–two completely different worlds separated by only eighteen city blocks. The severity of the scenery-change was a bit maddening for me. And so, my friend on the other end of the cell phone didn't understand why I had left the club. "I had to leave," I told him. "I have work to do. It's nothing personal toward you. Thanks for the invite."

So, there I was, standing at the base of this mammoth road at the bottom of the south pit. It was the only exit road to and from the hole and I felt guilty every time I walked on it. My fellow New Yorkers were trapped underneath and I couldn't wait until the road would close and the new military exit bridge would open. I could not shoot for the moment; I was humbled by this graveyard that sat on already hallowed ground. Closing my eyes, I talked to the victims in prayer and expressed how sorry I was. I have never had such an incredible appreciation for life than at that moment. I mean, come on, I had the luxury of being alive. I had hand warmers and I was dressed warmly and I could go home and eat if I wanted. I could jump on a bus and go anywhere I wanted. I could even walk to Central Park, sit on an old bench, and look at the trees if I so desired. These were all simple things to many, but great honors for me as I stood in front of this giant dirt road filled with hundreds of people who would never have those privileges again. They were taken away at the hands of cowards on September the 11th.

When I opened my eyes, I realized I needed to preserve this moment so that the world could see it through my eyes and, hopefully, feel what I was feeling. I backed up twenty feet (6m) to size it up and decide how to capture the image (see page 175) before I made my exit. At that moment, an FDNY Battalion Chief walked up to the spot I had just been standing in, removed his white Chief's helmet and said a prayer. In front of him in the rubble, hung a flowered wreath, placed there by a friend of an FDNY widow who had lost her husband in the collapse. This image of the Chief in prayer would be the victim's testament. I shot a few frames and then watched him walk away. Overwhelmed with emotion, I froze up inside. I looked around me and saw a few firemen digging and an ironworker cutting beams. I had a realization of the oddity of where I was and what I was doing with my life at that moment. I suddenly flashed back to my childhood on my Illinois ranch. I thought about when the first camera was placed in my hands by my mother, when I was a thirteen-year-old boy. As I dug my frozen fingers back into the now-warm gloves, I looked up to the high edges of the hole that surrounded me and then back at the hallowed road, and I thought to myself, "What am I doing here? Why me?"

The youngest of five kids, I grew up in the Chicago area suburbs of Highland Park and Barrington Hills. I had many hobbies, the most important being the art of getting into trouble at my father's quarter horse complex. At age seven, while playing with matches near a large garbage can, I nearly burnt my father's beloved complex down. This would be my first meeting with firemen—might I add, an unpleasant one—until many years later. That same year, my horse complex privileges now limited, my father, Morry, enrolled me in a martial arts program in order to harness my "creative energy." That proved to be a mistake: after four years I developed a fondness and talent for fisticuffs, both in and out of school.

At the age of eleven, while spending one of many days at home suspended from school, I became fascinated by an antique camera my father kept in his bedroom closet. Although it didn't work, I would regularly take it apart and wonder how this object could record images. I then started spending many hours each week studying award-winning *Life* magazine photographs in a *Best of Life* book we had in the house. I was amazed at how a camera could stop a moment in time and take me right into historical events. I wasn't born when John F. Kennedy was killed and laid to rest, but there I was with the photographer, watching little J.F.K., Jr., saluting. I was there with the photographer as Martin Luther King, Jr., lay dying on a terrace in the South. A young female napalm victim ran naked down the street in Vietnam and I was a witness. I was slowly learning the importance of the role of a photographer in freezing time so that future generations could learn from the past. Months later, I would later learn the basics of this art from a pinhole camera that was inside an issue of *World* magazine for kids.

Soon I began shooting on a small 110-film camera, not knowing that my mother, Sherry, was watching my curiosity grow. After getting rolls of family film back, she would often say, "Did you shoot this sunset, Gary?" or, "Who took this nice photo of the lake? Is this your photo, Gary?" I always assumed that everyone shot just like me, but I guess I was wrong. On my thirteenth birthday, my mother summoned me to her room. "The room" was serious business in my house, so I figured I was in for a lecture on how my fist-fighting in school needed to stop, or to find out which camp in Siberia she and my father were planning to send me. Instead she had a large box wrapped in paper. It was my birthday present, but she explained that it was a "special present." As I tore the paper off, a shiny box was revealed and in it was a beautiful Canon AE-1 35mm camera. It looked bigger than I was! As I stood there speechless, she explained that she loved my photographs and felt that I had a special talent that needed to be nurtured with a good camera. I was shocked that she thought I was doing something special when it came so naturally to me and I thought nothing of it. And so, the fighting quickly tapered, while my dogs, cats, horses, and insects gradually pulled the focus of my attention becoming my little unsuspecting photographic subjects on the ranch. I finally had a new hobby.

Consumed, I taught myself time exposures, macro photography, lighting, types of film, and anything else I could learn. One year later, a friend of my mother's suggested that I enter one of the many photos I had amassed in a regional photography show. At age fourteen, the youngest entrant by fifteen years in the show, I was awarded two blue ribbons. Three years later, at age seventeen, in my last year at Barrington High School, I won the local, regional, and state scholastic photography competitions, and my work was flown to New York City, where I won the prestigious Kodak Medallion and two Gold Key Awards. However, none of this would be important or relevant for me to write about were it not for the significance of where my winning photographs were judged and displayed in New York City. This would all happen at the World Trade Center.

FDNY Deputy Chief Bob Busch

FDNY Deputy Chief Ron Spadafora

September 7, 2001, was a great day for me. I was finally coming off my crutches after having had knee surgery performed six weeks earlier by Dr. Hans Paessler, a well-respected surgeon in Heidelberg, Germany. Up until the surgery, I was able to shoot fashion photography and celebrity portraits, but a knee injury had shut down my acting career and I needed to have the operation if I was going to get back into things professionally. I looked forward to getting through the next few months of rehab so I could begin auditioning again in early January. Everything was planned out. I had missed most of the summer and was looking forward to walking in Central Park without crutches that weekend to enjoy the Indian summer. I was not scheduled for physical therapy again until September 11.

September 11. Morning. Lying in bed, I had barely opened my eyes when I heard fists banging loudly on the door to my loft. I nearly had a heart attack as I jumped out of the bed, glancing at the clock, which read 9:20 A.M. I didn't answer at first because I was disoriented. Was someone trying to break in? As the next round of fists began, I heard, "Gary! Gary! Are you in there?" I recognized the voice and, peering through the hole, I saw it was my neighbor Darryl. He was an easy-going guy, I had never seen him get worked up. However, his wife, Cheri, was due to give birth that day so I knew what was going on. He was in a panic—she was probably in labor.

As I fidgeted with the door locks I thought I heard the words "World Trade" and "terrorists." I opened the door to hear, "Gary! Get up to the roof! Terrorists have attacked the World Trade Center!" My first reaction was, "Yeah, right, are you kidding me?" He replied, "I'm not kidding! Grab your camera and get up to the roof!" And so, I grabbed my Mamiya medium-format camera and some film and ran up to the roof, half dressed and feeling very uneasy. As I opened the door to the roof, I walked out into one of the nicest, sunniest mornings I can remember. However as I turned right, I saw Armageddon. Eighteen blocks away, the World Trade Center Towers were spewing black smoke into the blue sky. I felt sick to my stomach as my neighbors told me what had happened.

For thirty minutes we watched as the cloud of black smoke—and the number of floors it engulfed—quickly grew. I could only pray for the people on the plane and the workers on the floors where the plane had entered. I knew they were gone as I asked myself, "Who could do something so evil?" I would shoot periodically and then just stop and stare, feeling so helpless and not in control. At 10:01 A.M., my neighbor ran up to tell us that a plane had crashed into the Pentagon and yet another had crashed in a field somewhere. We knew we were under attack. Terrorists had attacked our beloved country. At 10:02 A.M. the South Tower disappeared in a cloud of smoke in fourteen seconds and the Wall Street area filled up with smoke. "Oh my God!" screamed my neighbors, as I stood silent. I could not believe what was happening. What about the people in the buildings? Or the people on the street below? These were the thoughts racing through my head. Then I rushed down to a restaurant where I was scheduled to meet a friend for breakfast at 10:00 A.M. Perhaps she didn't know what was happening and was waiting there for me? She wasn't there. I turned to race back as a plume of smoke hovered above the skyline, visible even from the street. The people near me had no idea what had just happened. I shot a quick photograph and headed back to the roof.

It was now 10:28 A.M., and as I leaned over the railing and stared at the remaining Tower and thought about the precious lives it held, something signaled that more evil was to come. The North Tower swayed slightly to the left and then back upright. The windows of the top twenty floors burst from the compression of the structure and were thrust like bullets into the air. We could clearly see the windows flying in the air, glimmering like silver fish as they caught the sun. I knew the Tower was going to come down and I looked at my camera. I had one frame left and I knew I had to shoot the collapse, as painful as it was. The Tower began its collapse from the very top and spread down like a waterfall, horrific in its perfect downward symmetry. I would shoot the last frame as the Tower was one-quarter of the way down, just seconds before it disappeared behind the other buildings. From where we were, as the Tower collapsed lower, we could see the hollow core that had housed offices—and precious human life—for the last thirty years. This new void in the skyline was frightening. Only ninety minutes before there were people working in that very airspace. Sick to my stomach, I reloaded and shot a few more color frames after the collapse and left the roof.

FDNY Chief Ron Werner

Thirty minutes after the collapse I went to Ground Zero to shoot. However, I wondered, "Do I really want to shoot? I mean, why?" I was traumatized already, and what was the purpose of shooting? I wasn't going to sell anything. For a moment, I considered not shooting anything, but then I realized that I had a job to do. All photographers have a responsibility during an historical world event like this to try to capture emotionally moving images so people around the world can connect. I would later learn that a photographer tragically died while trying to document the Towers on fire. His last words to his wife were, "It's okay. Don't worry. I'm with the firemen." Moments later the South Tower came down on him and the firemen. His camera and the last images he recorded were later found and preserved. Nevertheless, I would do my best and try to document this period for future generations. I walked right into the disaster zone without anyone stopping me and then began shooting, but after a few frames my immune system had other ideas. I had an anaphylactic allergic reaction to the chemicals in the air and as my throat slowly began to constrict, I feared I

FDNY Captain Steve Geraghty, who lost his older brother Chief Ed Geraghty on 9/11.

would die. I made my way to the doctor and spent the next few days getting Benadryl shots and intravenous vitamin drips. The doctor warned me to stay away from Ground Zero, but I didn't listen and got sick again. After learning my lesson, I decided to focus on documenting the city's reaction to 9/11 and only went to Ground Zero periodically until my system calmed down from the chemical exposure. I put up a website, SeptemberEleven.net, so people could see what was happening in New York, but I never had a clue where this journey would take me.

Once the smoke calmed down in November, I spent more time shooting near the pile to document for the SeptemberEleven.net website. Still, I was not allowed to go into the hole. I never sold any of my images; everything was for the website. It was now December and I decided there was nothing left to shoot, unless I was able to shoot in the hole. This would never happen, however, since recovery workers were the only people allowed in there. I had heard of photog-

raphers getting arrested for sneaking in and that was not for me. It wasn't so important that I needed to break the law, and besides, I needed to start focusing on my theatrical career. I decided that I would shoot my last images of Ground Zero, which were of the Christmas tree, post them on the website, and end my project. Toward the end of December I would discover that fate had something else in store for me.

It was more boredom than anything else that led me to read through the newspaper a second time that day in December. I was on the Long Island Railroad and needed to pass the time until I got to the doctor in Hicksville, Long Island. It was in that second reading that I caught a small article about sick firefighters from the early days of 9/11 who suffered from fatigue and respiratory problems. They were having the same symptoms that I had experienced in the early days and it angered me when I heard this because I felt I knew what was wrong with them. They had become chemically sensitive from exposure to toxins at Ground Zero and their immune systems were weak. Once in Hicksville, I asked Dr. Gary Jean-Baptiste and Edward Persaud of the prestigious alternative medicine center Medical Network of Long Island how they would feel about treating a handful of sick firemen for free as a kind of contribution to the relief efforts. Believing they could make a difference, they said yes, so I called the organization listed in the article, the Uniformed Firefighters Association (UFA), and explained to Manhattan Trustee Rudy Sanfilippo why I felt this special center could help and that the treatment would be free of charge. Mr Sanfilippo gladly said yes.

Only weeks later, the UFA was very happy when some of the men started seeing relief from the symptoms that had plagued them. They had indeed become chemically sensitive and their lung capacity was diminished, but as treatment began, some of their symptoms began to lessen. In conversation one day with Mr. Sanfilippo, he asked me if I had a photo of the Christmas tree from Ground Zero, as he heard I did some documenting there. There was a woman in California he wanted to send the photo to as a thank-you for the gift of gingerbread cookies she had sent to the firemen in New York. I directed him to the website and told him to tell me which tree photo he wanted. He called a day later to tell me he felt the site was very respectful and non-exploitive and that it paid homage to the FDNY. He asked if I was still shooting and when I informed him I had no access to the hole, he discussed the possibility of having me document the recovery on behalf of the UFA and UFOA, provided I would adhere to strict guidelines. Those guidelines included: don't shoot human remains, share a percentage of any of my future proceeds with a 9/11 charity, and most importantly, not to release any images to major media outlets until the last week of Ground Zero. He didn't want to wake up and see my photos from the hole in the papers every day. The focus of the job was not to sell my images for profit during the recovery, but to document for the website, for 9/11 families and for future generations. Also, I would have to fund myself for everything. I agreed with his guidelines, but I was in too much shock to fathom the shoes I was about to step into. There were no photographers allowed in the hole. Period. Except one. And that one would be…me?

I will never forget the first day in January when I rode into the hole on the gator. Driving down the South Exit Road, I was both physically engulfed by the hole and emotionally overwhelmed by the history of those seventeen acres (7ha). To say I was in shock is an understatement. It was like driving straight into the Grand Canyon, only this was a world filled not with beauty, but with construction workers, firefighters, rebar wire, beams, mud, drop-offs, massive trucks, and police officers. It was culture shock to say the least; this would be my new home for the next five months and I was the rookie here. The fact that I had a camera also threw off the men at first when they saw me coming. "Yo, no pictures! Put that away!" I would hear as I carried this large Mamiya camera in my hand. A friend of mine who was established down there acted as my guide and informed everyone that I was "okay." I was slowly introduced to the various FDNY Chiefs in different parts of the pit and began shooting in certain sections for hours at a time. In my early days of documentation, I would shoot portraits of firemen and come back the next day with 8×10 prints for them in frames donated by the Bodum store. It was a great way for me to contribute instantly and artistically, and it made them happy to have a memory of their time served. What I didn't realize was that all the time I was doing this for them, they were actually taking notice of me. I had figured they were too busy to remember who I was a day later. What I didn't take into account was that these were firefighters. They were a different breed. They cared. They remembered. They took notice. I would soon find out that it was my random acts of giving that would slowly earn me their trust and lead them to adopt me into the "brotherhood."

In the following pages, you will see my journey into Ground Zero and the recovery period. While the early days are also documented here, this book focuses on the recovery. You will see many special people that I had the honor of working with in the hole. You will see the inner workings, the tender moments, the tough moments, the highly restricted areas, the rough terrain, the late nights, the early mornings, the ever-changing scenery, the heroes, and most importantly, the love. You will see images that come from thousands of hours of living and shooting in the hole. Many days I didn't know the time or day. That was called Ground Zero time. I would often say to myself, "I need to go home and sleep for a few hours." However, leaving meant there was a chance I would miss history, so I usually stayed. I sometimes spent entire days down there without shooting so much as a single frame. It was the greatest test of patience and discipline I have ever known. This was a labor of love for me, although I pondered walking away several times because it was too much to bear. I am not experienced in wartime photography, nor am I a paramedic. There was no training for this and hiding behind my lens lasted only so long. I admit it was tough, but I felt compelled to tell the story of the men and women that I now look up to and admire. I shut down emotionally as best I could and prepared for a long haul. Like the men beside me, I would deal with my emotions at a later date. I never thought I would use later in life all the little photography tricks and tools I learned as a boy in Illinois, but Ground Zero certainly put all of my talents to the test. As a photographer, it was indeed a challenge.

This book is my contribution to America, and my goal is to help people connect and have a deeper understanding of the human spirit. I was placed in an important position and did my best to treat this role with respect and dignity. God bless all the volunteers who gave of themselves to make us smile and put food on our plates. You came from all over the United States with one goal in mind: to help. The ironworkers, the grappler/crane operators, labor workers, and Department of Sanitation workers were among the other unsung heroes that were silent, yet worked around the clock to help in the recovery. Although the photographs in this book are a result of my eye, it is the firemen who were instrumental in making many of them happen. I cannot put into words how the FDNY men that I now call friends have helped me. Your kindness and support enabled me to find my place there and feel comfortable enough to focus on my work. Thank you for allowing me into your world and letting me share in the most sensitive of life's moments with you—especially walking in the Honor Guard. Thanks for trusting me enough not to turn around when you heard the camera click away; you trusted that I was always "doing the right thing." At times I felt five inches tall when standing near you, yet you always made me feel like one of your own. While the city slept, you dug tirelessly through the mud and rebar wire with the hopes of bringing someone home to their family. I regret I did not have the honor to work with the relatives of lost civilians at the World Trade Center, however, I did have the privilege of working alongside the FDNY men who lost their sons, brothers, and fathers. I watched you search quietly for months filled with good days and bad days. You showed up, never complained, and went home covered in mud. Yet, no matter what each day brought, somehow you never lost your cool and always kept your dignity. I respect all of you in the FDNY more than you will ever know. The last days of Ground Zero were tough—but then, the whole journey was hard. The realization for thousands of people that their missing loved one would not be coming home was the wrong ending. Some of those people I had worked with for months. It was now personal for me and their disappointment was mine also. Each day I hoped that the families of the civilians, the police, and the firemen that I worked with would have some kind of closure. On the last day, Firefighter Ralph Geidel said to me, "I wish it was last September again just so I could have another chance to find my brother." It was May 30 and Ground Zero was finished. An era was over. We cried and hugged and looked into the empty cement hole for the last time. We would miss each other; the bond we had subconsciously formed was now clearly evident as the glue that had held us together during all those months. I walked away and passed security for the last time, with that lump in my throat, trying hard not to look back. In the last week of Ground Zero, I would release my images and my story to the *New York Times*. On May 28, 2002, the story ran, entitled "From a Camera at Ground Zero, Rare Photos of an Agonizing Dig."

In this book you will see some portraits of firemen who lost loved ones. These shoots were very emotional and many tears were shed. The courageous firemen in these images wanted to pay tribute to all the fallen and wanted all the people of the world to connect on a deeper level. Personal items were brought out one last time before being stored away forever and I thank those men for this honor. While I couldn't photograph everyone who lost a loved one on 9/11, I feel deeply that these men's portraits and stories are representative of all the loss of life that occurred, whether they were civilians or uniformed service personnel. A special thank you to President George W. Bush, not only for trying to keep us sane during a time of turmoil, but for your constant fight against terrorism so that the events of September 11 will never be repeated. We must never forget the real heroes of 9/11: the people who died. I hope this book is a tool of healing for all in the same way working at Ground Zero helped to heal me. While the terrorist attacks temporarily shook my faith in humanity, working with the men and women of Ground Zero helped to restore it. As FDNY Father Chris Keenan once said to me on a cold January day after prayer service, "Gary, two bullets went into the World Trade Center, but only love came out." God Bless America and Never Forget.

—*Gary Suson*
New York City

OPPOSITE: The first photograph taken September 11, 2001, at 9:30 A.M., from my roof in the Meatmarket District. My reaction upon seeing the sunny, blue skies was quickly overshadowed when I turned the corner on the roof and looked downtown, only to see the smoke billowing out of the World Trade Center. It was surreal and the memory still makes my stomach turn. At first, I denied the thought of the obvious. However, there was no mistake—the United States was under attack.

RIGHT: September 11, 10:03 A.M. As we watched the horror unfold at the World Trade Center, a neighbor ran up to the roof to tell us that a commercial airliner had just crashed into the Pentagon. While we listened to what she was saying, the South Tower collapsed and the Wall Street area filled with smoke. I turned and took this photo seconds later. Resembling an effect on a movie set, the ash quickly rolled towards us, cutting through the buildings and streets. Seconds later, an F-16 fighter jet thundered overhead toward the World Trade Center area. We were now living in a new world.

PAGE 14: At around 10:10 A.M., I left my roof and ran around the corner to Pastis, the restaurant where I was scheduled to meet a friend for breakfast at 10:00, before this tragedy stopped time. She was not there, so I assumed she'd seen the news on television. As I turned to head home, I saw a massive smoke cloud from the South Tower collapse hovering in the sky, visible even from the ground in the Meatpacking District, eighteen blocks away. As I shot this image, I realized that the people on the street had no idea what had happened. They carelessly walked to work, oblivious as to what was going on. One man asked what I was shooting and thought I was kidding when I told him. I raced back to the roof of my building.

PAGE 15: September 11, 10:28 A.M. As I leaned against the roof railing, staring at the North Tower, I saw the building sway to the left and all the windows began popping out, shooting glass far into the air. I checked my camera and realized that I had only one frame left. The tower was on its descent—about one quarter of the way down—when I took this photo. Twelve seconds later, the North Tower was gone. It happened very fast.

LEFT: September 11, 10:30 A.M. After the collapse of the North Tower, the Wall Street area was engulfed in smoke. Watching from my roof in the Meatpacking District, I could only imagine the madness going on down there. The sick feeling at watching this was only heightened by the fact that it was a beautiful, sunny morning with blue skies. This was the last photo I shot from the roof until later that night, at 11:45 P.M.

OPPOSITE, TOP LEFT: One hour after the World Trade Center collapsed, people gathered around a portable TV on the roof of a car off 9th Avenue to hear the latest news.

OPPOSITE, TOP RIGHT: September 11, 10:00 P.M. On the West Side Highway bicycle path that leads toward Ground Zero, two volunteers spent hours tearing bed sheets into temporary face masks before leaving to hand them out to rescue workers.

OPPOSITE BOTTOM: September 15, 2001. Crowds gathered on the West Side Highway to cheer the rescue vehicles as they entered and exited the World Trade Center site.

LEFT: September 11, 11:45 P.M. New York City's first night without the World Trade Center as part of the skyline. I shot this photo from my roof, leaving the shutter open for several minutes to record the searchlights and the smoke that rose from the site.

ABOVE: September 12, 1:00 A.M. The West Side Highway was closed to traffic, except for emergency vehicles. I jumped over the medians to set up on the other side for a multiple exposure. This photo is about six exposures on a single frame. Streaks of light are recorded from the dozens of passing ambulances and squad cars on the way up from Ground Zero. The white trailers behind are refrigerated temporary morgues that housed the victims. In the far right corner is the smoke from Ground Zero, illuminated by the searchlights. This photo, for me, captures the frenzy that went on all through the night.

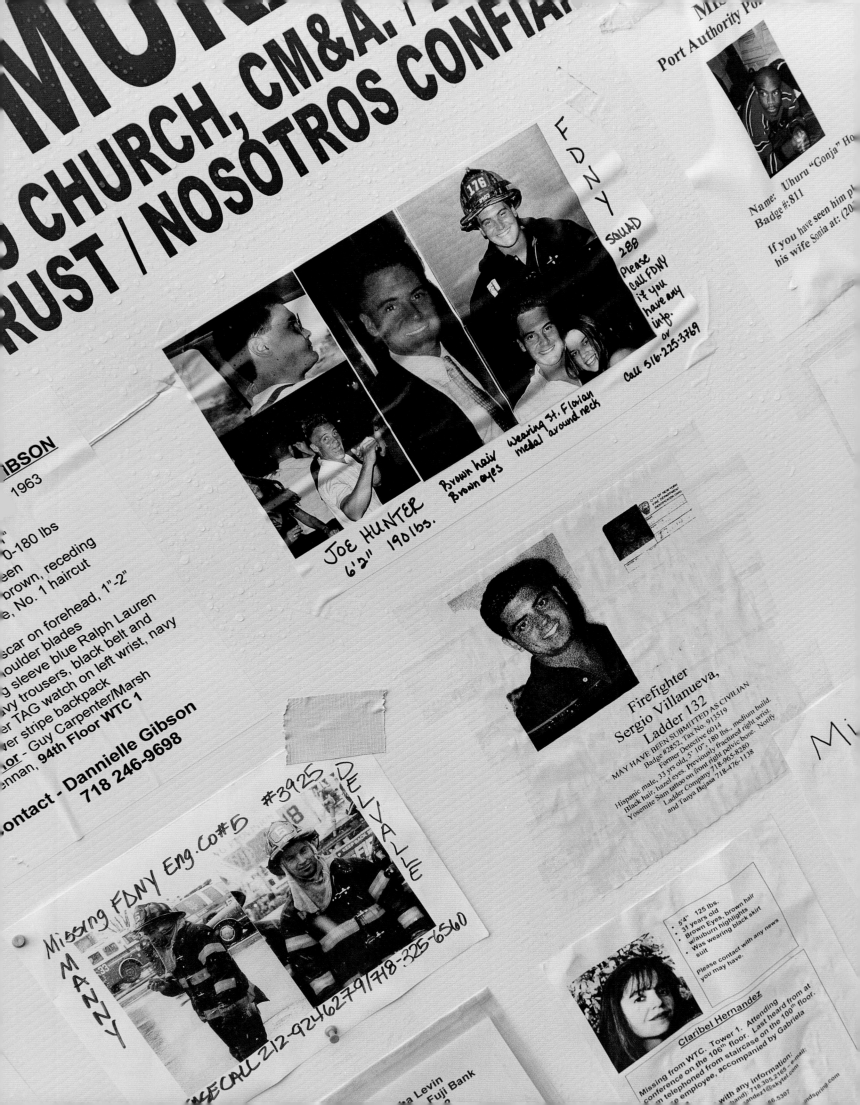

MUT...
...D CHURCH, CM&A, ...
...RUST / NOSOTROS CONFIA...

Mi...
Port Authority Po...

Name: Uhuru "Gonja" Ho...
Badge #: 811

If you have seen him pl...
his wife Sonia at: (20...

...IBSON

1963

...0-180 lbs
...een
...rown, receding
...e, No. 1 haircut

...scar on forehead, 1"-2"
...oulder blades
...g sleeve blue Ralph Lauren
...vy trousers, black belt and
...er TAG watch on left wrist, navy
...ver stripe backpack
...nan, - Guy Carpenter/Marsh
...or - **94th Floor WTC 1**

...ontact - Dannielle Gibson
718 246-9698

FDNY
SQUAD 288
Please call FDNY if you have any info.
or
Call 516-225-3769

JOE HUNTER   Brown hair   Wearing St. Florian
6'2" 190 lbs.   Brown eyes   medal around neck

Firefighter
Sergio Villanueva,
Ladder 132

MAY HAVE BEEN SUBMITTED AS CIVILIAN
Badge #2852, Tax No. 913519
Former Detective 6014
Hispanic male, 33 yrs old, 5' 10", 180 lbs., medium build,
Black hair, hazel eyes. Previously fractured right wrist.
Yosemite Sam tattoo on front right pelvic bone. Notify
Ladder Company 718-965-8280
and Tanya Bejasa 718-476-1138

Mi...

Missing FDNY Eng.Co#5   #3925
DELVALLE
MANNY

CALL 212-924-6279/718-325-6560

- 5'4"   125 lbs.
- 31 years old
- Brown Eyes, brown hair
  w/auburn highlights
- Was wearing black skirt
  suit ...

Please contact with any news
you may have.

Claribel Hernandez
Missing from WTC. Tower 1. Attending
conference on the 106th floor. Last heard from at ...
...telephoned from staircase on the 100th floor,
...n employee, accompanied by Gabriela

...with any information:
...band): 718-305.2165 – e-mail:
...ahndez1@skytel.com

...ia Levin
Fuji Bank

OPPOSITE: "Missing" signs were put up all over Manhattan. Families and friends of people who were known to have been working in the World Trade Center that September morning waited and prayed that they would hear good news. Firemen, EMS, NYPD, and PAPD who responded to the call were now missing also. Whatever street you were on, there would be posters like these bringing you face to face with strangers that, all of a sudden, you were praying for.

ABOVE LEFT: September 12, 2001. A prayer vigil forms at Union Square; people of every creed and color join hands and form a circle. They recite the words, "May peace prevail in...," going through every country in the world, from A to Z. Here, they all say, "May peace prevail in Swaziland."

ABOVE RIGHT: September 13, 2001. Outside the Chelsea Market on 9th Avenue, two volunteers prepare to take hot food down to the Ground Zero rescue workers. The tragedy of September 11 brought out the very best in all of us as we rallied as a nation.

RIGHT: A New York State trooper checks IDs for people living below 14th Street. Police personnel of all types and from all over New York were brought in to help.

OPPOSITE TOP: A photographer grimaces in disbelief at one of the many "Missing" posters that adorn a pole in Union Square.

OPPOSITE BOTTOM: Neighbors gather on 8th Avenue for a candlelight vigil on September 12.

RIGHT: At the "Mural of Hope" in Union Square, a woman reads a poster of one of the missing.

MURAL OF HOPE / MURAL DE
EL CAMINO CHURCH, EMAU
IN GOD WE TRUST NOSOTROS

WE SHALL
RISE AGAIN

ABOVE LEFT: A moving tribute in candles and photographs at Union Square. Seeing personal photographs that were most likely removed from family albums made everything hit home. Those who were missing were not just numbers on a list, but unique individuals with families, friends, and aspirations.

ABOVE RIGHT: This NYPD officer's face reflected what I think everyone in the United States was feeling: despair, anger, and pride. "New York's Finest" really came through on September 11.

LEFT: One thing about the events of September 11 and the days after: you could see the pain and emotional fatigue in everyone's eyes. You didn't have to look hard. This Parks Department officer's eyes spoke volumes to me. She emerged from Ground Zero covered in that horrible white soot. This was one of the few photos I purposely blurred with slow shutter speed, jerking the camera and using soft focus to create the sense of motion and uneasy tension during this period. Sometimes these shots fail; I am very glad this one worked.

OPPOSITE: Union Square, "No Words" shrine. Seeing this note, written in oil paint and surrounded by roses, candles, and photographs, made tears come to my eyes for the first time. It got to me because ever since the tragedy I had been searching for words to make sense of it all. I kept looking for some answer that never came. This note helped me to understand that it was okay to feel the way I did—emotionally overwhelmed and speechless.

ABOVE: December 11, 3:30 A.M. The Christmas tree that was erected at Ground Zero right in front of the steel WTC facade brought comfort to the workers and honored the memories of the fallen. It was the most beautiful tree I have ever seen—a bright light shining inside a zone filled with many bad memories. Notice the miniature World Trade Towers to the left of the tree.

RIGHT: December 2001. Inside the restricted area, a large Star of David was erected near the Christmas tree as a tribute to all the Jewish victims of September 11.

BELOW: Inside the Ground Zero site, an impromptu FDNY Command Unit had been established in a small wooden shack. This touching memorial was set up just outside. Two chains had been welded together to form a cross; a long-stemmed rose and a photo of a fallen firefighter were added at the top. At the base of the cross rests a letter that broke me up when I read it one freezing and windy night. It was written by the daughter of a lost fireman who asks her daddy to please come home. Lights from a small Christmas tree glow in the background.

ABOVE: In the early days of the recovery effort, when the dust and smoke were at suffocating levels, rescue workers went through air tanks by the hundreds. Here, a stack of used air tanks awaits removal from the site.

LEFT: "American Disaster." One of the many Red Cross areas set up around the city where medical supplies and food were made available to the rescue workers.

BELOW: A new team of search and rescue workers arrives at Ground Zero.

RIGHT: At Ground Zero, a truck pulls up carrying search and rescue teams ready to begin an all-night battle to find victims and possible survivors. It was like a war zone.

PAGE 32: Two fire trucks pulled from the rubble lie in the shadow of the facade of the World Trade Center as smoke rises off the pile. Firefighters would regularly walk over to the trucks and quietly say prayers in memory of their fallen FDNY brothers, who rode in them for the last time on September 11.

PAGE 33: This is one of the most difficult and emotional photos I've ever taken. As I was moving toward this demolished fire truck, some firefighters approached. Out of respect, I put my camera away. One of the men leaned against the truck and proudly dusted off the FDNY emblem. He then removed his gloves and scrawled the word "Why?" in the white ash. I've never had a bigger lump in my throat than at that moment. After the men left, I shot this photograph.

LEFT: This is Ground Zero—a war zone. As the sun was setting on the first Sunday after the attacks, Old Glory blew in the wind. Silhouettes of once great structures— and the memory of the people who made them come to life—loom amid the ash. This picture reminds many people of photographs taken of bombed-out France during World War II. As I paused to take this photograph, a Battalion Chief approached me and asked if I had seen the area at night. He said that the remaining facade of the North Tower looked like hands folded in prayer when the spotlights hit it. What is eerie about this photo for me is that there are three crosses in it: one on the far left, one on the far right, and a third likeness on the facade in the center.

ABOVE: In an example of the many types of agencies that came together during this time of crisis, an NYPD officer shakes hands with a National Guardsman.

ABOVE: Days after the Towers collapsed, I would make my first trip into Ground Zero. The facade of the North Tower was always a head-turner because it was the last piece of the World Trade Center standing. Becoming its own entity, the shining silver facade was almost beautiful in its refusal to fall down. Although it was sad to see it standing all alone, it was also inspiring, because it allowed us to see a piece of what was once an incredible structure, very similar to the awe of seeing Stonehenge. On a sad and reflective day in December 2001, when the facade was finally cut down, Ground Zero would be forced to take on a new identity.

ABOVE: Another angle of the facade at night, a few days after the collapse. Steam rises off the pile and the facade looks centuries old. It was inconceivable to think that less than one week earlier this charred shell had been the financial center of a busy metropolis.

LEFT: It was my first trip into Ground Zero, just days after the terrorist attacks. The fire trucks that had been destroyed were lined up near what used to be Vesey Street. Firemen had walked over to the rigs, which were caked in white ash, and scrawled notes in memory of their fallen FDNY brothers. Here, on the side of what was left of Ladder 18's truck, the messages speak for themselves.

ABOVE: No car that was pulled out of the rubble ever looked like a car. They were twisted, crushed, and sometimes fused together. Five months after the attacks, this car dashboard was pulled out from forty feet (12m) down in the rubble.

LEFT AND OPPOSITE:
Outside Squad 18 on West 10th Street, an elderly woman lights a candle in memory of the fallen firemen (left), and a man gently places a rose on the memorial created for the men lost from this firehouse on September 11 (opposite).

ABOVE: October 2002. "Late Shift." In the early morning hours, an NYPD officer, with the shell of a destroyed WTC building in the background, walks past a security fence filled with hundreds of cards and flowers left by mourners.

RIGHT: In Manhattan's Meatpacking District, I noticed two record release posters on a wall. Both albums were scheduled to be released on September 11. The poster with Mariah Carey embodied so much happiness, the exact opposite of what the 11th turned out to be. It should have been a normal New York day—a beautiful sunny morning, appointments, lunches, dinners, Broadway shows—but it wasn't. The record companies removed these posters two days later.

glitter
MARIAH

Glitter, the new soundtrack and motion picture featuring the smash hits "Loverboy" and "Never Too Far"

featu

N STORES SEPTEMBER 11   IN S

43

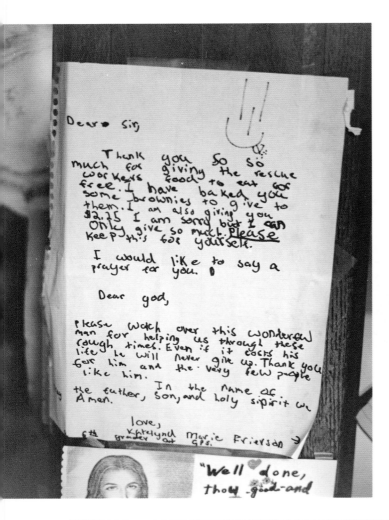

ABOVE LEFT: Walking into Nino's restaurant for lunch one day, I saw one of the many heartwarming letters from children. This letter, written to Nino by sixth-grader Katelynd Marie Frierson, was an example of the children's innocence that brought tears to the eyes of many workers. It reads, "Dear Sir, Thank you so so much for giving the rescue workers food to eat for free. I have baked you some brownies to give to them. I am also giving you $2.25. I am sorry but I can only give so much. Please keep this for yourself. I would like to say a prayer for you: Dear God, please watch over this wonderful man for helping us through these rough times. Even if it costs his life he will never give up. Thank you for him and the very few people like him. In the name of the Father, the Son, and the Holy Spirit we pray, Amen."

ABOVE RIGHT: Restaurant owner Nino with two of New York's Bravest on Canal Street in October. Nino fed thousands of Ground Zero workers for free in the months after the attack.

LEFT: At Nino's restaurant, one of the many volunteers from across the United States who donated their time serves a police officer a hot meal.

RIGHT: A visit from Britain. Fire Chiefs Dave Smith (left) and Dave O'Dwyer (right) of the Hereford and Worcester Fire Brigades traveled to Ground Zero from England in January 2002 to lend a helping hand. With them they brought the hundreds of thousands of dollars in donations they had collected, which they gave to a September 11–related charity.

BELOW: Angels come in many forms. A group of us were sitting and eating in Nino's restaurant, which served free food to rescue workers, when in walked two little angels. The girls, who were sisters, had come with their mother all the way from Texas to sing songs for the workers. Listening to them sing, with their little red, white, and blue angel wings flapping around on their tiny backs, made us all smile. For the moment, we forgot about the indignities we were seeing that day in the hole.

LEFT: January. One of my first official trips into the hole as archive photographer for the Uniformed Firefighters Association. It was so overwhelming that I almost couldn't shoot. The landscape was surreal, with giant caverns, steep drop-offs, and muddy hills filled with snake-like rebar wire. The knowledge that many people were still trapped under it all was as disturbing as seeing the Towers collapse months earlier.

ABOVE: I shot this picture on my first entry into Ground Zero in September 2001. Crushed, ash-covered cars sit piled on top of one another. It was disturbing to see such chaos. Little did I know what I would see later.

LEFT: As I entered the world of Ground Zero in January 2002, the first thing I noticed was the intense wartime feel in the hole. Everyone was divided up into teams that were dedicated to different tasks. Everyone was so focused and driven. In my early days of documenting, I spent more time studying the system and meeting the men than shooting. Here, four firefighters jump off the gator to go to work digging in an area.

OPPOSITE: Engulfed in smoke, a Ground Zero ironworker burns through a large piece of the South Tower facade that is buried in dirt. The unique pungent chemical smell that was given off when the beams were burned was enough to instantly remind me to put my gas mask on.

RIGHT: Volunteer recovery worker Michael Bellone's mud-caked face and clothes express perfectly how raw it was down the hole. It was common to change clothes halfway through a shift if the conditions were harsh, as it was on this rain and mud-filled day. Bellone, whose mother and father both passed away within a 3-month period during the recovery, assisted firefighters with recoveries and volunteered in the FDNY's A.T.V. unit from September 11 through the closing ceremonies on May 30, 2002.

RIGHT: New York City firefighters, refusing to give up the fight to bring home the missing, rake through the dirt and rubble.

OPPOSITE: It was a cold Sunday evening in February when I met firemen Ralph (left) and Mike Geidel during a shift change down in the hole. I asked them why they were not on dinner break. After all, the hole was empty and nothing was going on. They explained that they, along with their father, Paul Geidel, were searching for their brother, Gary Geidel, who was a fireman from Rescue 1 and had been missing since September 11. Shift change was their preferred time to dig—it was quieter and more private. This solemn time on the hallowed ground of the site allowed them to feel closer to their brother, whose photograph Ralph wears on his helmet.

RIGHT: When I asked the Geidel brothers how they knew exactly where the Towers once stood, they quickly pulled out and unfolded a map of the former WTC layout. Here, Ralph points to where they think their brother, Gary, might have been when the North Tower collapsed. Ralph, a gold miner residing in California, left his West Coast home in September to come to New York to search for Gary along with his brother, Mike, and their father, Paul.

LEFT: The first few days of January 2002. I wasn't yet allowed down into the hole when recoveries were made, so I stayed on the outer edges and shot. Here, at about 4:00 A.M., in the middle of the hole, a firefighter is found and the men crowd around to assist in recovering their fallen brother.

ABOVE: An arctic night in December 2001, around 5:00 A.M. Silhouetted by the searchlights, an NYPD officer stands guard near one of the entrances to Ground Zero.

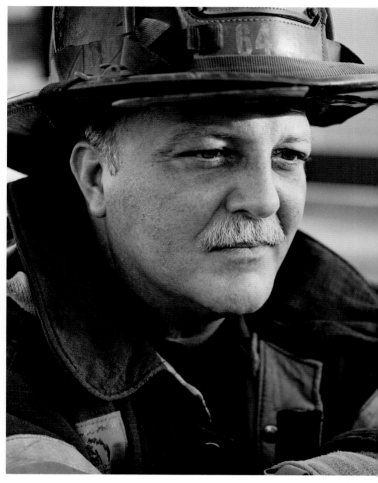

LEFT: Having access to all areas of Ground Zero meant that I had a better chance to tell the full story and to show aspects of the site that people would otherwise never see. There were so many pieces needed to complete the photographic puzzle, and this one happened by accident. It was pouring rain in January 2002 and I wasn't able to shoot in the hole. I went up to the roof of the Ladder 10, Engine 10, (10-10) firehouse, which overlooks the site. Many heroes from this firehouse lost their lives on the morning of September 11, and it was now shut down and used as a command center and supply shed for the firemen who worked in the hole. After seeing the destruction from this disturbing angle, I peered over the back edge of the roof and saw two welders on a platform working the cutting station despite whipping cold rains. Their job was to cut the rebar wire down before the trucks could leave the site. Unless the conditions were very severe, Ground Zero never slept.

ABOVE: Firefighter and union delegate Rudy Sanfilippo, the Manhattan Trustee for the Uniformed Firefighters Association who was elected to oversee and protect the rights of Manhattan's firefighters. Rudy is also the reason why there's a photographic record of "The Recovery." He wanted 9/11 families to have a photographic record of their loved ones being recovered and fought to put me in Ground Zero as the *Official Photographer* for the U.F.A. Rudy was also one of the lucky few who narrowly survived the collapse of both towers on September 11.

LEFT TOP: FDNY Deputy Chief Joseph Pfeifer, who was the first to arrive and set up command when the planes went in to the World Trade Center, cradles the American flag that was used to cover his brother Kevin's body when he was found in the North Tower area and carried out on February 3, 2002.

LEFT BOTTOM: Deputy Chief Joseph Pfeifer holds items that are very special to him and his family. They belonged to his brother, FDNY Lieutenant Kevin Pfeifer of Engine 33. On the left is Kevin's fireman's badge, which coincidentally had the same badge number as Joe's first fireman's badge. On the right is Kevin's Lieutenant's shield. Chief Pfeifer pointed out to me that the badge number, 1513, has much significance to him religiously. He explained that the Bible, in John, chapter 15, verse 13, reads, "Greater love hath no man than this, that a man lay down his life for his friends."

RIGHT: It was Sunday, February 3, 2002, and people around the country were watching the Super Bowl. I came into the 10-10 firehouse inside the Ground Zero site to warm up, eat, and watch the Super Bowl halftime show. Meanwhile, Chief Joseph Pfeifer, who had played a large role in the rescue operations at the World Trade Center when the planes first went in, was at his firehouse doing paperwork. The football game was about to begin when over our receivers came the words that Joe's younger brother, Lieutenant Kevin Pfeifer of Engine 33, had been found in the North Tower area. Chief Pfeifer got the call at his firehouse and raced down. It was one of the very first Honor Guards I would document. As I stood on top of the 10-10 firehouse, shooting in the freezing cold, a group of firemen visiting from Florida stood to my right, overflowing with emotion at seeing firsthand the results of the worst terrorist attack ever on American soil. As I heard the chaplain's prayer come over the receivers, I set my camera down to salute two American heroes. Chief Joseph Pfeifer proudly and bravely walked his younger brother Kevin out of Ground Zero.

LEFT: FDNY Captain Mike Banker of the Special Operations Command Unit confers with Nick Demassi of the FDNY ATV Unit during work in the hole.

OPPOSITE: A photo that makes me proud to be an American. With the Stars and Stripes leading the way, firemen push up a steep mud- and wire-filled incline to bring a civilian home. On the left side of the photograph, a fireman grasps his brother's hand as he tries to get his footing.

RIGHT: If you had to go into battle, FDNY Chief Steve Rasweiler is the kind of man you would want leading you. Tough but always fair, Chief Rasweiler was always recognizable by his bright royal blue helmet. He was always in the thick of every operation and watching him work was like watching a World War II field general. It's no wonder he commanded the respect of everyone he worked with. To the left, firemen use hand signals to direct the grappler operator as to where to dig next during a long recovery.

ABOVE LEFT: A stokes basket sits in waiting during the first hours of the opening of the South Tower road in March 2002. Everyone was prepared for many recoveries once the road was opened. The first recovery, shown in progress here, happened in the first forty-five minutes of digging.

ABOVE RIGHT: A firefighter stands guard over a fallen brother near the treads of the grappler that helped free him during a recovery. The grappler operators were so skilled that they turned the manipulation of the giant steel claws into a gentle, delicate art form.

OPPOSITE: The first hour of the opening of the South Exit Road brought a number of recoveries. Here, a firemen who bears the names of his fallen brothers on his back, uses the "sawzall" cutter to get through the annoying rebar wire en route to freeing a victim.

LEFT: February 2002. With the newly constructed military bridge and massive Ground Zero site in the background, the workers of Ground Zero line up on the South Tower Exit Road and salute a fallen hero being marched out of the hole with honors.

ABOVE: The very last Honor Guard on the South Tower exit ramp, before it was closed down. The chaplain and chief make their way toward me as I fire off a few frames. I rarely shot more than a few photographs during an Honor Guard; then I would put my camera down and salute.

ABOVE: FDNY Chief Steve Zaderiko, eyes closed and head bowed, holds out his handy talky for a chaplain who says a prayer for one of several civilians found on a busy spring day at Ground Zero. Chief Zaderiko was one of many firemen who would come down to the hole to help as soon as they finished work on their regular FDNY shifts.

RIGHT: South Exit Road, February 2002. Ground Zero comes to a halt as a fallen fireman begins his journey home. The Honor Guard always made our emotions run high. In the background, the last remaining piece of the military bridge to be installed sits on the ground.

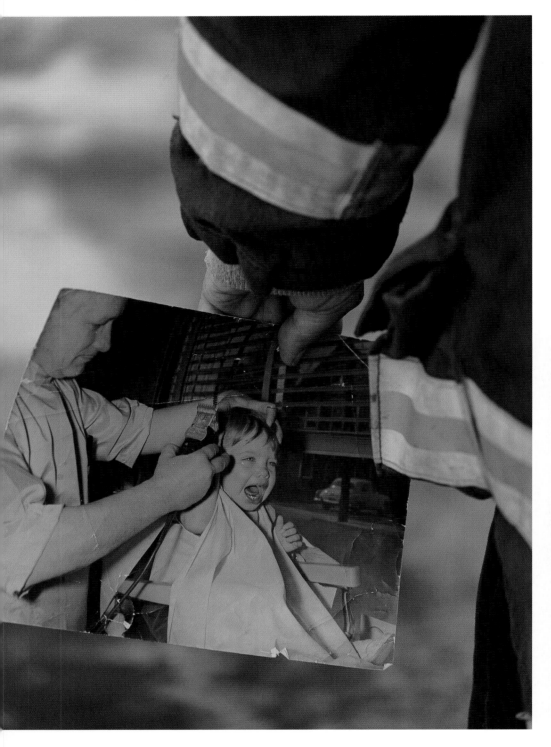

OPPOSITE: It is not unheard of in the Fire Department to have families of firefighters that go back decades. Sons often grow up wanting to be firemen just like their fathers, as is the case with the Geidel family. There is one fireman missing from this photo to make it complete. His name is Gary Geidel, an Eagle Scout, former Marine, and decorated Firefighter with Rescue 1. Gary was lost on September 11 after running to help out at the World Trade Center on a day when he was scheduled to be off. He was due to retire seven weeks later, after twenty years of service. His father, Paul Geidel, a Korean War veteran and a retired Lieutenant with Rescue 1, stands here with his sons Michael, also of Rescue 1 (left), and Ralph, a retired FDNY fireman.

ABOVE: When I decided to photograph the portraits of the fathers, brothers, and sons of fallen firemen of September 11, I made it my goal to keep the memories of their loved ones alive through my images. Many of the men brought special photos or objects that were important to them—objects that would help keep the memory alive. Paul Geidel brought a treasured photograph of his son taken during young Gary's very first haircut. The photo looks like it was taken out of the *Life* magazine archives. Paul liked the photo because "Gary just looked so cute with those big, blue eyes.... At the time, it was the worst fear that he had—getting a simple haircut. But he conquered that fear and went on to accomplish many more important feats as he got older. But it all started at this haircut."

ABOVE: Retired FDNY Lieutenant Paul Geidel of Rescue 1. Paul is a combination of compassion, toughness, and humbleness. A son could only hope to have a father as proud of him as Paul Geidel was of his son Gary. I worked for months with Paul down in the hole and he was an inspiration to me. It was his sense of humor that carried him through the really tough days—always looking at the lighter side of life and staying positive. To watch him go through months of digging and never once complain made me take a second look at my own life and laugh at issues that I originally thought were problems.

OPPOSITE: This photo best represents the size of the machines used at Ground Zero. Two firemen, rakes in hand, and a Port Authority officer seem tiny against the backdrop of a massive earthmover.

RIGHT: Lee Jackson, a sixty-three-year-old ironworker from South Carolina, puts on a welding display in the South Tower area that caused me three burns in the process. However, the sparks thrown off by his torch created a magnificent display, like the Fourth of July. Later, he explained to me that thicker beams yielded more sparks than the smaller beams.

ABOVE: At the transfer station, firefighters take a five-minute break while the dirt they have just sifted through is dumped into a truck to be carted away to the Staten Island landfil for a final look. In the foreground are hundreds of remnants found in the rubble and put aside for removal. Victim's personal identifiable belongings, such as rings, watches, and I.D. were always turned over to the Port Authority Police to be later viewed by surviving families. Remnants, however, were either discarded or given to museums for educational purposes.

OPPOSITE: While many senior citizens ride on golf carts heading for the eighteenth hole, these long-retired firefighters sit on the back of an ATV cart, slogging through the mud and rubble of Ground Zero. Many retired firemen showed up at the site to volunteer their services, willing to do anything they could to help in the recovery efforts.

LEFT: On a Sunday morning in spring, two missing firemen are recovered and carried toward the military ramp, where everyone was lined up and waiting for the prayer and Honor Guard to start. Just moments earlier, as the firemen walked in my direction, I noticed that all the ironworkers had temporarily left their ten-foot-tall (3m) cutting station in the middle of the pit to line up on the ramp. I quickly climbed to the top of the scaffolding, which enabled me to capture the men marching past from a unique angle.

LEFT: Moments after a call comes through our handy talky receivers, firemen swarm around the body of a civilian and plan the best way to make the recovery.

BELOW: If this photo doesn't convey the heart of a firefighter, nothing else will. In March 2002 an injured firefighter, here saluting a fallen brother being carried in the Honor Guard, showed up at Ground Zero willing to do anything to help out in the recovery efforts.

OPPOSITE: A Ground Zero chaplain, marching in unison with the leaders of the Honor Guard, solemnly heads through the mud and toward me before turning left to enter the military bridge.

DARK PASSAGE

February 11, 2002. Crushed PATH train in subway tunnel. I walked on this train just a few days before this photo was taken. The train was almost perfectly intact, and in it I found ash-covered newspapers from the morning of September 11. I felt as if I had been transported back to 9/11 in a time machine. I had an uneasy feeling while in the train. It was one of the scariest places I had ever been, and there was no guarantee of safety. Days later I came back to enter the train again, only to find that the entire overhead concourse had given way and had crushed the train like a tin can. This crushed car was my wake-up call that being down here was no game. I would have to choose my areas to shoot carefully—and get out quickly. Everything was unstable, with fault lines running throughout the substructure. However, I wanted a close shot of this train and said to myself, "People have to see this. If I don't shoot it, who will?" I lowered myself down to the slippery, rubble-filled tracks and left my bag on the dark platform, taking only a flashlight and my camera. With my rubber rain boots on, I slowly waded in toxic water up as far as I could go before logic told me to stop. It was so intense that the photo almost doesn't do it justice. I could also not escape the presence of a strong spiritual energy down there. I took the photo and got out quickly. Over the course of the next few weeks, I persistently asked a friend of mine at the site if anyone perished in the PATH train area, to which he always said, "No. Everyone got out of the subway that morning. Why do you ask?" I told him that there was a strong energy down there. This went on for weeks because it really bothered me, but he always gave me the same answer. Then, on my night off I got a call from my friend who told me not to speak, as he was going to put his handy talky up to the receiver so I could listen. I listened in amazement to the crackling voices of the recovery team saying that a victim had been found in the PATH train area, near a subway car. The victim was found approximately twenty feet (6m) in front of where this photo was taken. I felt my face get cold and I told my friend I had to hang up.

LEFT: Outside the PATH train station, mud-covered tracks disappear into the rubble.

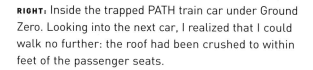

RIGHT: Inside the trapped PATH train car under Ground Zero. Looking into the next car, I realized that I could walk no further: the roof had been crushed to within feet of the passenger seats.

LEFT: One of the many surreal and terrifying sights in the demolished PATH train area, now reduced to almost a crawlspace. I needed my flashlight to figure out that these were turnstiles sticking out of a six-inch (15cm) -deep slippery pool of mud and ash that reeked of burnt wood. Bricks and ceiling tiles stick out of the mud and, toward the back, the ceiling hangs only a few feet over the turnstiles. As I turned to leave, I tripped and fell on what turned out to be a woman's purse that had probably been dropped in the frenzy of that morning.

ABOVE: One of the lead PATH train cars sits trapped in a web of twisted steel and concrete.

LEFT: PATH train area. Inside the Commuter's Car bar, seventy-five feet (23m) under Ground Zero. The liquor bottles behind the bar had been toppled like bowling pins, and a charred martini glass and ice-scooper sit where they had been left the night before. Shooting inside this bar involved more than just walking in. Broken glass, jagged steel, and scattered furniture had to be slowly and carefully maneuvered around to finally get to this area toward the back of the bar.

RIGHT TOP: Smoky, ash-covered liquor glasses dangle in midair and the cash register key hangs as it did the night of September 10, when the bar manager closed up and went home for the evening.

RIGHT BOTTOM: The instability of the areas I walked in under Ground Zero is aptly demonstrated in this photo. A few days after I photographed the Commuter's Car bar, I returned to shoot for a second time only to find that the floor underneath had collapsed, leaving the entire bar hanging on the side of a cliff. The glasses still hang eerily in midair.

OPPOSITE: Retired FDNY Firefighter Lee Ielpi cradles the helmet found near his fallen son, Jonathan, of Squad 288, on December 11, 2001. Only about eight FDNY helmets were recovered at Ground Zero. Soft-spoken, kind, and always the perfect gentleman, Lee entrusted me with the honor of capturing this tender moment. Before we said goodbye, Lee told me, "I know my son is in better hands now, but I would rather have him in mine."

LEFT: FDNY Captain Bill Butler. Captain Butler lost his firefighter son, Thomas, on September 11. Although retired, Captain Butler decided in December that he was going to suit up and go down to Ground Zero to look for his son. He was a fixture there from that time forward and wanted only one thing: to bring Thomas home so he and his family could give him the farewell his hero son deserved. I worked with Captain Butler for quite some time, and his courage and determination really touched my heart and changed my outlook on life.

RIGHT: FDNY Captain Bill Butler at Ground Zero, rake in hand, looks toward where the Towers once stood. One night, as I was standing at the edge of the hole, I watched an FDNY widow weep as she waited to hear if her husband had been found. Most of his company had already been found and she hoped her husband, one of only two still missing, would be recovered next. When the news came that it wasn't her husband, she cried heavily. At that moment, Bill Butler walked up and embraced her as she cried on his shoulder. We heard Bill say, "I know your pain, I lost my son Thomas. It's going to be okay. We're going to bring your husband home. I promise." Bill, despite his own pain, gave of himself to help another. The next day her husband was recovered. She walked up to Bill after the Honor Guard and hugged him. Bill said, "I told you we were going to bring him home." She replied, "But what about Thomas? I want you to get your son home." Bill said, "Don't worry, his day will come." Bill's son was one of close to two hundred firefighters who were never recovered.

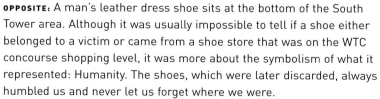

OPPOSITE: A man's leather dress shoe sits at the bottom of the South Tower area. Although it was usually impossible to tell if a shoe either belonged to a victim or came from a shoe store that was on the WTC concourse shopping level, it was more about the symbolism of what it represented: Humanity. The shoes, which were later discarded, always humbled us and never let us forget where we were.

ABOVE LEFT: North Tower area. A radio used either by in-house security or by WTC engineers/maintenance sits in the rubble next to a torn and water-damaged business card holder. The cards were from businesses located on various floors of both the Towers.

ABOVE RIGHT: Bent keys on a makeshift wire key chain sit in the dirt. They most likely belonged to a WTC maintenance worker.

LEFT: Digging in a "hot spot" in March. The best places to dig first were areas that were known to have stairwells.

RIGHT TOP: Down in the trenches, digging with the men. A rake, some gloves, and some hope: it was as rudimentary as you can get.

RIGHT BOTTOM: As primitive as one can imagine, pieces of wood were nailed together with chicken wire to speed up the sifting of dirt in search of remains.

PAGE 92: Port Authority Police Officer Cronin digs. I remember one morning in February. I hadn't left the hole in thirteen hours— I was done, exhausted. (You kind of have to stay, because you never know what each minute might bring.) An FDNY Chief I knew was near me, digging. I asked if it would be okay if I helped, and he told me to grab a rake. "There's no method, Gary. Just find a spot and dig." So that's what I did. No computers, no technical training, no maps— just pick a spot, dig, and hope. I was so honored that he would let me dig alongside him. It was somewhat disturbing, as you would imagine, but it felt good to be able to help in a different way than I had been accustomed to. It was that morning, when I was on my knees digging, not knowing what I would find, that everything seemed to come together for me. It gave me a deeper understanding and respect for the men and women I had been photographing all those months.

PAGE 93: The sun rises on a January morning as massive grapplers, resembling prehistoric animals, move dirt and debris. It was about ten feet (3m) to the left of where I stood to take this picture that I would later find a torn and charred page from the Bible, which would give me the strength to continue my photographic duties despite the horrors I was exposed to.

LEFT: On Tuesday, March 12, 2002, retired FDNY Firefighter John Tipping showed up at Ground Zero. As he walked in, he noticed that his son-in-law, an NYPD officer, was on duty. As he went to say hello, he asked if there were any recoveries being made, to which his son-in-law replied, "Yes, I think they may have found John, Jr." John Tipping, Sr., raced down to the hole and discovered that his missing son had been found. After taking a few private moments to be with his son, he carried John, Jr., out of the hole with the help of his son-in-law and the men of Ladder 4, Engine 54, the firehouse where John, Jr., had proudly served.

ABOVE: FDNY Chief Steve Rasweiler, a fixture at Ground Zero, consults with the medical examiner during a recovery.

LEFT: In March 2002, a preacher, small in stature but big in heart, stands near a fallen firefighter, preparing to say a prayer as six fireman stand guard. He paused to find a verse in his Bible, earmarked a page, lowered his arm, and here he waits for the Chief to order the beginning of the solemn moment of prayer. I refuse to allow hate to permeate this photo- graph. I see only love. If you are starting to feel what I felt at Ground Zero, then you are begin- ning to understand how love and brotherhood dominated the seventeen- acre (7ha) site.

OPPOSITE: March 2002. Despite the fact that life had gone on outside the hole, as symbolized by the towering buildings in the background, Ground Zero was its own little world that had not changed. On a day where people in those buildings were probably drinking cappuccinos and having business meetings, in our private world, a chaplain says a prayer over a fallen fireman as Deputy Chief Ron Spadafora holds the handy talky out for him.

PAGE 98: Mud drips off the boots of the men in the Honor Guard as they proceed to the military ramp, where everyone prepares for the salute. My heart was heavy every time this sacred ritual was performed.

PAGE 99: Honor Guard salute. A brotherhood of FDNY men who lost their firefighter sons and brothers salutes a recovered fireman. Second from right is Lieutenant Dennis O'Berg, third from right is Captain Bill Butler, fifth from right is Ralph Geidel, and sixth from right is Lieutenant Paul Geidel.

SITE: FDNY Chief Steve Zaderiko. When Chief Zaderiko's thirty-day tour was over
e end of January 2002, he continued to come to Ground Zero on his days off and
work to help in the recovery efforts. I was also guilty of never resting. It was hard
st when you knew that your job was unfinished. No matter how many times we
d say to our concerned friends, "We're fine," the fatigue and psychological drain was
thing that our eyes could never hide. The daily pressures took their toll on all of us.

LEFT: Reverend Brian Jordan is a Franciscan priest who ministered to the workers
ound Zero. Every Sunday morning he held an emotional service under the giant
"WTC Cross," which was two steel beams in the shape of a cross that had fallen
the 67th floor and landed upright. To attend this service, only thirty feet (9m) from
lace where nearly three thousand people died, was a very moving experience.

ABOVE RIGHT: In January 2002 I had the pleasure of meeting Father Chris
Keenan, the new FDNY Chaplain. He introduced himself with, "Hi, I'm the
new Probie." Keenan succeeded the beloved Father Mychal Judge, who
was killed on September 11 while giving last rites to a fallen firefighter.
He knew Father Judge well and though it was a big task to step into his
position, Father Keenan quickly won the hearts of the firefighters with
his kindness and sincerity. I was attending the funeral of the mother of a
Ground Zero rescue worker in Brooklyn when, out of the blue, in walked
Father Keenan, who delivered a beautiful eulogy and sang a touching
prayer. This rescue worker had lost his mother in the middle of watching
the CBS television documentary about September 11 at a special room
at Ground Zero. When Father Keenan heard of this, he found out where
the funeral was to be held and showed up. It was a Sunday morning,
after services, when I was feeling down after watching a recovery, when
Father Keenan said, "Gary, two bullets went into the World Trade Center,
but only love came out. Remember that." I took this portrait of Father

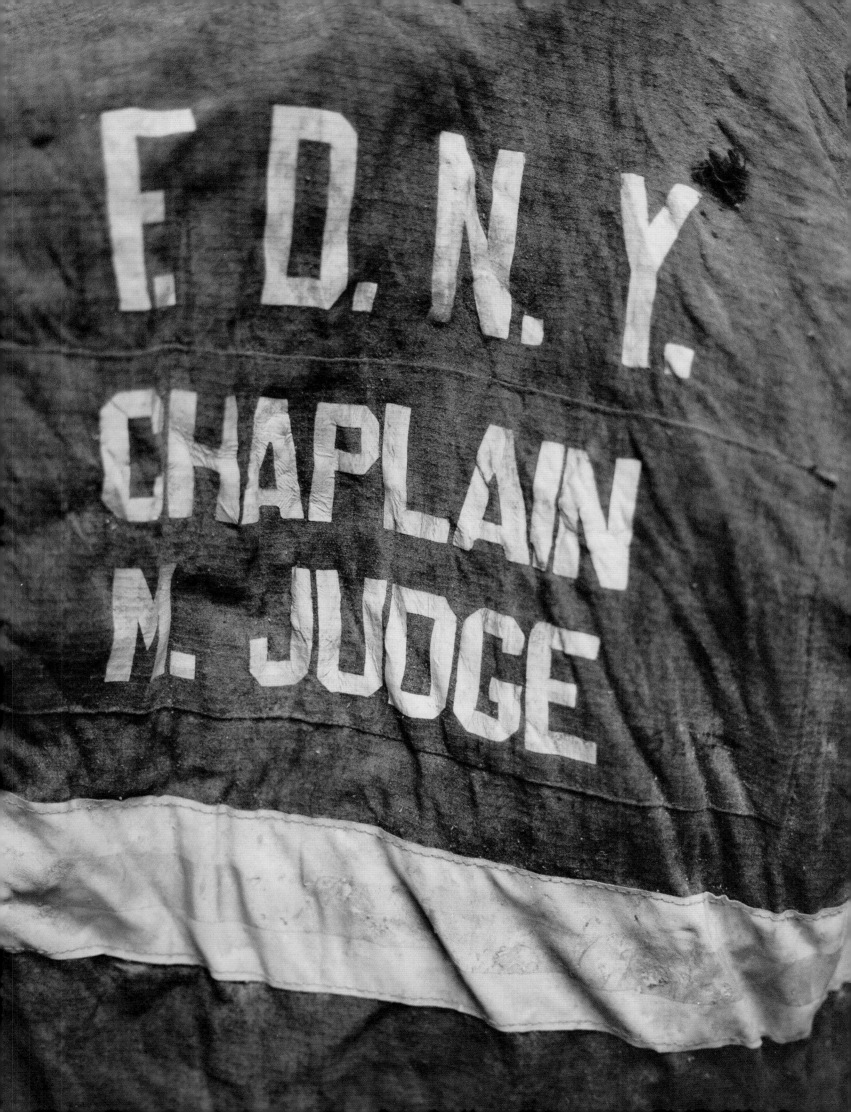

MYCHAL'S PRAYER

Lord, take me where You want me to go;

Let me meet who You want me to meet;

Tell me what You want me to say, and

Keep me out of Your way.

OPPOSITE: One of the most moving memories I have was when FDNY Father Mychal Judge's turnout coat was uncovered in the rubble of what had been the South Tower lobby. It was found in March 2002 and the jacket brought silence, awe, and comfort to those who saw it. It was very special for me to see—and even more special to hold—the dust-filled jacket in my hands for those few moments. It was, and is still, beyond words....

ABOVE LEFT: One night my friend said, "Gary, jump in the gator. I'm taking you up to meet the man who found the famous Ground Zero cross." And so off I went, up the muddy hill to meet Frank Silecchia, a laborer with local 731. On the third day after the attacks, Frank had discovered an enormous iron cross sticking out of the rubble. It had fallen from the 67th floor and landed upright. The cross was erected at Ground Zero and brought hope to all at the site. Frank once said to me, "Touching people's hearts is the most amazing thing about finding the WTC cross. We should never forget our faith."

ABOVE RIGHT: The massive "WTC Cross" at Ground Zero. Every Sunday at 10:30 A.M., a prayer service was held underneath the cross. It was attended by Ground Zero workers who found comfort in prayer. It was the reason Ground Zero's nickname was "God's House."

OPPOSITE: A seven-hundred-pound (318kg) bear hug. On the left is Frank Silecchia, the man who found the "WTC cross." On the right is Mike Bellone, a rescue worker from day one. Mike and Frank met in December 2001 and bonded when Mike's father passed away that Christmas Eve. On this cold Sunday morning in January, Mike was supposed to join Frank and me at this site for the regular Sunday prayer service held by Father Brian Jordan under the massive cross. But Mike, who hadn't slept in two days, was suddenly called away to assist in the recovery of a fireman. When the service was over, Frank let me scale the ladder to take a closer photo of the cross. As I got up to the top, I turned to tell Frank that I hated heights. Just then, Mike pulled up in his ATV and got out. Frank saw that Mike was emotional and gave him a big, long hug. It was one of the most touching things I have ever seen.

OPPOSITE: Ironworker Keith Russell, on his dinner break, burns a Star of David and several crosses into a World Trade Center beam. Religious keepsakes were regularly cut, upon request, and given to Ground Zero firemen, police officers, and victims' families.

ABOVE AND RIGHT: Aloha New York! It was quite a surprise when the State of Hawaii, through Tim Farley and Lt. Governor Mazie Hirono, delivered five thousand leis and six thousand pineapples, courtesy of Dole and airfreighted courtesy of United Airlines, to New York City. The beautiful purple and white hand-made leis were given to all Ground Zero workers on Easter Sunday; they really lifted everyone's spirits. Fireman Gibby Craig of Squad 41 (above) wears one of the leis.

A MESSAGE IN THE ASHES

It was the last few days of January and I was standing near the North Tower area conversing with an FDNY Chief, when I noticed some charred papers on the edge of a steep incline. Separating me from the papers was a Jersey barrier, erected to keep workers away from the dangerous drop-off. I asked the Chief if I could photograph the papers and he hesitantly said yes, but asked me to make it quick because it was dangerous. I shot only three frames. The first was of a charred letter from police headquarters. Barely sticking out from under the letter were some cream-colored papers. When I lifted the police letter, I found there were a few wet and charred pages from a Bible. The Bible itself was nowhere to be found. I was instantly taken aback by this find, but never had a chance to examine the pages because my coworker pulled up in his gator and told me to jump in, as there was a recovery in progress that we had to get to. I leaned over quickly, shot two photographs, and jumped in the back of his gator. That night there was a huge rainstorm and Ground Zero turned into a giant mud pit and had to be temporarily shut down because the trucks couldn't make it up the hill.

The next day I got the proof sheets back and nearly fell off my chair when I saw that the passage on the page facing me was Genesis 11, the Tower of Babylon. It was a very moving, though bizarre, find; I took the symbolism of the "11" and the "Tower" as a positive sign that God was watching over the victims in their last moments, and that He was also watching over this hallowed ground during the recovery efforts. Also, I found the page during a period when I was considering tapering off my shooting, because the things I was seeing were too much to bear. I am not trained for wartime photography and the sights that go along with it. This was a war zone and it was taking its emotional toll on me. Finding the Genesis 11 Bible page gave me the strength to continue with my duties; I felt someone "upstairs" must have approved of what I was doing. Whether it was just some strange coincidence or divine intervention, it had important meaning to me. A group of my friends went down to look for the page the next day but it had been washed away into the mud during the storm. I wish I had grabbed the page at that moment, but I was so rushed that it slipped my mind. At least I have it recorded on film.

ABOVE: A mud-soaked teddy bear recovered in the North pit sits defiantly on a Jersey barrier wall. I thought the bear was symbolic of our great country. We were temporarily caught with our guard down and were hurt, but we are still standing—now stronger than ever.

LEFT: Broken glasses and case, South Tower area. It was always items like this pair of glasses that grounded me as to where I was. Remnants always hit home for me, no matter what they were. Even though these glasses were found sealed in the case to the left and were most likely from the optical shop on the concourse level, it matters more about what they remind us of. While we will forever see video images of the Towers crumbling, we can never forget the humans that were inside. We never saw them in their last moments, but the remnants may help us to connect and thus always remember and appreciate the beauty of human life.

ABOVE: In between where the South and North Towers once stood, a green toxic pool filled up the middle of the hole when cracks in the slurry wall began allowing the Hudson River to leak in. The pool was siphoned out over the course of a week.

LEFT: It was a windy winter night and I was exiting the hole when something blowing in the wind at the base of the North Tower ruins caught my eye. I walked over and saw a teddy bear, flowers, and a "Happy Birthday" balloon tied to a string and weighted down with stones. It put a lump in my throat: it was the first time I had seen this small memorial, and I knew there must be a story behind it. I would later find out that an FDNY fireman had been recovered in this very spot. Weeks later, on his twenty-ninth birthday, his widow asked a friend working in the pit to put these items in the exact spot where he was recovered.

OPPOSITE: It was March when I met FDNY Lieutenant Gregory Fodor while he was digging in the North Tower area. I was changing film as we struck up a conversation, and I learned that he was searching for his missing brother, Lieutenant Michael Fodor, Jr., of Ladder 21. The Fodor family is rich in American history and patriotism. He revealed to me that his father, Michael Fodor, Sr., was a Navy man. "My dad was at Pearl Harbor when the Japanese bombed it. He was assigned to the submarine base and was on a small boat in the harbor called a motor launch the morning the attacks took place. The Japanese planes flew right over his head. Miraculously, he survived." Greg's brother Michael and the six men of Ladder 21 he rode down with to the burning Towers were never found. From September 11 through March, Greg searched diligently. On many occasions, firefighters who worked with Michael have told Greg that his brother was the best boss they ever had. "My heart goes out to all the families of the people who were lost. My brother Michael died for the people of New York City and did so doing what he does best: fighting fires."

OPPOSITE, TOP: In the enormous relief tent, known as "the Bubble" to the workers, a Salvation Army worker cleans up after one of the many thousands of people who passed through here daily to eat their meals. The workers in the Bubble were known for their constant emotional support of the men who walked in exhausted and hungry. The smiles that flowed regularly from the volunteers' faces warmed the hearts of many men before they had to return to a world filled with hardware and backbreaking digging.

OPPOSITE, BOTTOM: St. Paul's Church, located just one hundred yards (91m) from the hole, became a safe haven for hungry and tired rescue workers, who could go there to get help from volunteer chiropractors, massage therapists, and podiatrists. This is Rich Jimines, a chiropractor from Michigan, giving a free adjustment to a fireman. Even at 3:00 A.M. there would be a chiropractor waiting to volunteer his time and skill to make the rescue workers feel better.

ABOVE: Ground Zero was a little community set up to take care of its recovery workers. Here, a worker in the giant relief tent cleans the floors near the showers.

RIGHT: A wash-down sign at one of the many entrances to the site.

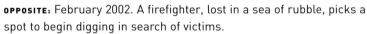

OPPOSITE: February 2002. A firefighter, lost in a sea of rubble, picks a spot to begin digging in search of victims.

ABOVE LEFT: North Tower area. A designated area for personal effects found in the dirt. A work uniform/jumpsuit, most likely a spare that belonged to one of the many engineers and maintenance worker at the World Trade Center, is laid out near some broken gun fragments.

ABOVE RIGHT: A worker lowers his head for a moment as if in prayer, while a water truck hoses down a cloud of smoke that was stirred up by a grappler as it moved debris.

RIGHT: The Deutsche Bank building. The massive building that faced the South Tower was draped in a black cloth shroud because the facade had been ripped open when the collapsing Tower fell into it. Although the recovery effort at Ground Zero officially ended on May 30, 2002, the search for remains continued in the bank, which was the last uncharted area. The giant American flag at the top could be seen from two miles (3km) away.

OPPOSITE: A sign for the World Trade Center proudly rises from the rubble in February 2002.

PAGE 118: In March, I was standing five feet (2m) away from a powerful moment in history and I knew it. It is a strong memory for me. Six firemen, two of whom were retired, stand guard over a fallen FDNY brother. They waited silently and respectfully for the chaplain to approach and read a Bible prayer for a 9/11 hero.

PAGE 119: It was not an easy experience to photograph the Honor Guard. Although I was allowed to capture these historic moments, I never felt right about taking more than three photos because I felt that the sound of my camera was disrespectful. This time belonged to the fallen hero— not to me. I was given an incredible honor, and I was careful never to abuse it. Each fallen man was responsible for saving the lives of many civilians. The purpose of these images, and my mission overall, was to remind people of this. The silence during these solemn marches was deafening, broken only by the sound of the firemen's worn leather boots scraping the muddy, stone-laden exit ramp.

ABOVE: I was told when I began documenting Ground Zero that the clock in the PATH train station, which stopped at 10:02 A.M. when the South Tower collapsed and shut off all the electricity, had been removed. That frustrated me because I wanted to photograph it; I felt it was a non-living witness to the catastrophe. Over the course of two months of trips down into the PATH tunnels I saw many heart-stopping things. The spiritual energy alone down there was intense, not to mention the destruction. However, I always felt incomplete for not being able to shoot the clock for historical purposes. I knew it would never happen since I couldn't turn back the hands of time and make the clock reappear. It was March when I made my last trip down to the PATH train. The subway structure was becoming increasingly unstable, and I was told there could be no more journeys down there. I was on my way out of the tunnels for the last time when I passed by a room I had walked by dozens of times but never entered, as it just looked like a storage room for tools. This time something made me push the door open and go in just for the heck of it. I walked in and my flashlight found a workout bench and weights for the track workers to use on their lunch breaks. As I turned to exit, my flashlight caught something high on the wall that reflected strongly back at me. It was a plug-in clock, stopped at 10:02 and 14 seconds. There was a second clock! Completely shocked, I froze in my tracks and just stared. It was a very powerful symbol. So much life had tragically stopped in those last 14 seconds when the South Tower collapsed, and the clock just made it all hit home for me. I shot one frame and left the tunnels for the last time.

117

OPPOSITE: A moment etched in time—and in my memory—forever. I was standing a few feet away from the men during an Honor Guard in March 2002 when the chaplain began a prayer. In unison, the firemen bowed their heads in tribute to their fallen brother. It was painful, as would be expected. But the combination of the Stars and Stripes, the men beside me, and the honor of standing near this brave fireman who had given his life to save civilians made me proud to be an American.

LEFT: On a busy day for recoveries in March, the chaplain says a prayer for a fallen firefighter. He speaks into the Motorola receiver held by FDNY Chief Harten, whose eyes are closed in prayer. Fire Commissioner Nicholas Scoppetta stands at far left. It was always beautiful when the chaplain's words could be heard clearly through the receiver clipped to the shoulder of each firefighter's bunker jacket. All the machines were turned off and work came to a halt as the prayer echoed throughout the whole site.

RIGHT: I stood there amazed during the recovery of a civilian in March 2002 when a swarm of firemen, big in stature and even bigger in heart, acted gently and with great care as they tucked the American flag around a WTC hero.

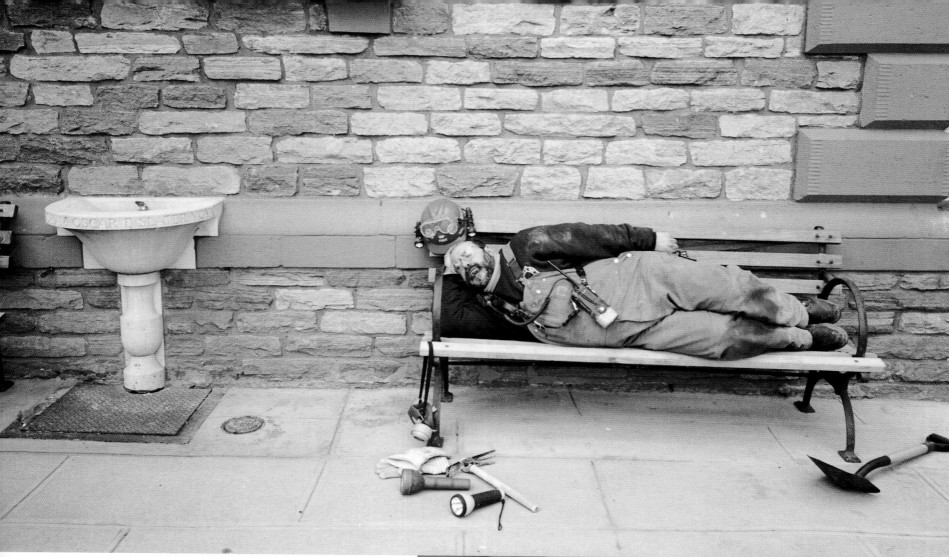

OPPOSITE TOP: Easter Sunday. Morning light beams through the stained glass windows, filling the historic St. Paul's Church with a beautiful, diffused glow.

OPPOSITE BOTTOM: February 2002. It was early one winter morning when I awoke in St. Paul's Church and saw a crew of firemen resting in the pews with their bunker jackets lined up in a row. The church, a safe haven for tired and hungry recovery workers, was always filled with supportive volunteers from all over the United States who wanted nothing more than to help the recovery workers feel comfortable on their breaks. In the background are some of the many signs and banners sent from around the country.

ABOVE: An exhausted recovery worker, his tools spread out around him, naps on a bench in the graveyard behind St. Paul's Church.

RIGHT: Letters of support from school children around the United States adorn every church pew.

LEFT: On a chilly night in February, I was escorted down to the third level of the Customs/Secret Service building. I was told there were charred cars I would have to see to believe. After walking down three dark stairwells that were barely lit with small bare lightbulbs, we arrived in the parking garage that housed government-issue vehicles. The sounds of dripping water echoed through the cavernous garage. As we walked, I was told what to expect but was horrified when I shined my flashlight into a black corner and saw a graphic display of charred cars, turned violently upward and sticking into the air like toys. If I hadn't been at Ground Zero, I would have thought I was looking at some bizarre display of modern art.

RIGHT, TOP AND BOTTOM: Time traveling. March. Six months after the attacks, a friend of the owner took me to a condemned apartment building across from where the South Tower once stood. Nothing had been touched since September 11. Covered in ash, the houseplants were dead, the furniture white, and mice scurried under hundreds of papers that had blown through the shattered windows. I was told that when the Towers started to collapse, the tenant who lived here ran and hid in her bathtub. The woman's sandal on the floor also came through the window.

LEFT: Meet FDNY fireman Tommy, a.k.a. the "Sock Nazi" of Ground Zero. When he wasn't busy assisting in recoveries, Tommy was the man responsible for putting everything from rakes and shovels to warm socks and gloves into the hands of workers in the hole. His supply shed was located in the 10-10 firehouse within the grounds of the World Trade Center site. Although Tommy was always keeping the men in high spirits with his comic skills, it was not advisable to walk into his tool shed without an invitation. The consequences could be dire. As Tommy once told me, "These donated supplies have a weird way of walking away on their own. If I don't guard them, they grow legs."

ABOVE: January 2002. FDNY West Command Center. Chief Jim Riches (center, seated) discusses the day's activities with his colleagues.

RIGHT: On an early morning in February 2002, FDNY Chief Guzman (left) and Chief McGrath map out the day's plans in the West Hut, a small wooden shack that served as the FDNY command center for the west side of the hole.

RIGHT: FDNY fireman Jimmy Riches, Jr., a former NYPD officer, was preparing to celebrate his thirtieth birthday with his family on September 12, 2001. Terrorists took that away from him on September 11, a day that his father, FDNY Chief Jim Riches, will never forget. March 25, 2002, is another day that Chief Riches will never forget. I had the honor of working with Chief Riches, known as "Big Daddy" by his friends, for many months at Ground Zero. I knew he had been looking for his missing son, Jimmy, Jr., ever since September 11, but we never really discussed it. He was usually quiet and deep in thought if he wasn't busy overseeing the day's tasks. Only once did he open up and tell me, "I want to be here and I know my son would want me here. There's no other place I should be. I know if I was missing, my son would be here for the long haul also." Chief Riches and his three other sons, Timmy, thirty, Danny, twenty, and Thomas, seventeen, spent March 25 attending his grandmother's funeral. She was buried on her ninety-fifth birthday, the same day as Timmy's thirtieth birthday. After the funeral, Chief Riches and his family decided to drive by his grandmother's house one more time. As he did, he received a call from Chief Dan Melia at Ground Zero. Jimmy, Jr., had been found. Later, as his three sons stood at the top of the pit, Chief Riches walked to the north pit to see his fallen son. On a day filled with more emotion than can be imagined, Chief Riches and his sons would walk Jimmy, Jr., out of the hole with honors. In this photo, Chief Riches, wearing his son's shirt from Ladder 114, holds his Battalion helmet alongside his son's helmet, which was found on March 25.

LEFT: One early morning in March, in the West Hut, I was warming up with some hot coffee when Chief Riches asked why I wasn't shooting. He laughed when I told him I was taking a break from the PAPD cop down in the hole that wasn't fond of my camera. So, Chief Riches, always the guardian, decided he'd walk with me down to the north pit. He spoke to me about his missing son along the way. It was the first time he had told me a little about Jimmy, Jr. As we walked up to the highest ridge inside the hole, he approached the edge, stopped talking, and leaned on his wooden rake. Twice I tried to start up some conversation, but he was very quiet. I gathered that he was deep in thought and wanted to be alone, so I told him I was going to go shoot. I walked down the other side of the ridge and looked over my shoulder. Chief Riches was still gazing out and leaning on the tool that had become synonymous with the hole. Something about the way he was standing on that ridge told me to shoot this frame. Three weeks after I shot this photograph, on March 25, Chief Riches' son was found ten feet (3m) below the very spot where he is standing in this photo.

A TWIST OF FATE

FDNY Captain Michael Donovan has a charmed life. Fate had put Michael three minutes from death when the voice of FDNY Chief of Department Peter Ganci changed his destiny. On September 11, Captain Donovan was assigned to Ganci's office at headquarters. He was scheduled to work on a special project the morning the planes went into the World Trade Center. The next thing Captain Donovan knew, he was standing outside the North Tower looking up at the smoke pouring out of the World Trade Center. He recalls thinking, "I gotta get into the building," but he had no gear.

As he turned to make his way into the nearby 10-10 firehouse to borrow fire gear, the second plane exploded into the South Tower above his head, and debris rained down on him. He ran directly to the fire trucks parked nearby, borrowed some gear, and suited up. It was now close to 10 A.M. and he was ready to go when he saw his friends Timothy Stackpole and Dennis Cross running by. He said that if they were going into the South Tower he would like to go with them. Tim Stackpole said they were going in at that moment and he was welcome to join them. Captain Donovan began walking toward the entrance of the South Tower with the men when he heard, "Mike, wait! Where are you

going?" He turned around and saw it was Chief Ganci. "I'm going up into the Tower," he told the Chief. "Stay—I have a job for you here." Chief Ganci told Michael to set up and man the radio transmissions coming out of the South Tower. Although Michael wanted badly to go in and fight the fire, he obeyed his order, set up, and began monitoring. Only three minutes had passed when Captain Donovan heard a Mayday call announcing that the

elevators were free-falling. He looked over to relay this information to Chief Ganci but only got as far as saying, "Chief, I'm getting a Mayday that..." when an enormous thundering noise was heard as the South Tower began to collapse. Captain Donovan looked up for a second and then ran for his life as debris fell all around him. He made a run for the down ramp of a nearby parking garage and was close to the entrance when the force of the collapse blew him twenty feet (6m) down the parking ramp. "It was like when you get taken by a strong wave in the ocean." He was now trapped with others in the dark garage, which was encased in rubble. Calling for other firemen, he led a group to a stairwell that miraculously wasn't covered at the top and escaped. After realizing that Chief Ganci was missing, Mike went back into the garage to look for him, only to find the Chief, disorientated, making his way out on his own. As Captain Donovan prepared to assist in setting up a new command post near the North Tower, Chief Peter Ganci, the man who was responsible for saving Mike's life, would perish as the North Tower suddenly collapsed at 10:28 A.M.

In the days after the collapse of the World Trade Center, hundreds of firemen assisted in the rescue and recovery efforts, which made identifying one's fellow firehouse members among the sea of black-and-yellow bunker jackets a hard task. In order to make it easier to identify colleagues from far away, codes were taped onto the backs of the jackets. As shown in the bottom photograph, Mike and the other members of his house taped POSA on the backs of their jackets, which stands for "Pride of Sheffield Avenue," the nickname of Engine 290, Ladder 103, in Brooklyn.

THE HAND OF FRIENDSHIP

Meet FDNY Lieutenant John Citarella (left) and his longtime friend FDNY Lieutenant Steve Turilli (right). They love to kid each other, as all friends do. One of their oldest jabs is the one the bigger-framed John has always given to the smaller-framed Steve, calling his hands "little girly hands." September 11 would change that. When the planes went into the World Trade Center, John and Steve were at Rescue School on Randall's Island, where they teach. They drove over to Squad 41 in Harlem, threw on some borrowed bunker gear, and sped down to Ground Zero. Moments later they were in the lobby of the Marriott Hotel, avoiding jumpers and getting orders. A Chief had just told them to go up to the 90th floor of the South Tower, which was smoking violently. Steve grabbed his gear and took a few steps toward the exit as John adjusted his gear. Only seconds later, an enormous roar was heard as the South Tower came down; part of it fell through the Marriott Hotel, burying Steve and John in rubble. Neither of them knew what had happened, other than that it was "something catastrophic." John had taken a step toward the wall when he heard the crash, and this is where he would be trapped under fifteen feet (5m) of rubble. With one knee pinned up and pressing against his chest, his arms pinned and his helmet pushed down over his face, he

heard and saw nothing and assumed if he wasn't dead yet, he was nearing the end. Meanwhile, the smaller-framed and agile Steve had managed to somehow wiggle his way out of his entombment. Steve's first instinct was to call for John, but there was no answer. With his flashlight shining he called for John again. John could hear Steve calling and was trying to scream but his voice was muffled and knew that no one would hear him.

But Steve did pick up the muffled scream under all that rubble and called out, "Johnny, is that you?" John yelled back, "Yes, get me out of here!" Steve couldn't understand the muffled voice so he yelled loudly, "John, if that's you, make noise! Bang something!" The only movement John could make was with his right hand, so it was sheer luck when that hand found a piece of metal. He started awkwardly swinging it and it banged up against a piece of steel beam. Steve followed that noise and began frantically moving heavy debris as the noise got louder. He burrowed into the debris, handing back pieces of concrete to Chief Larry Stack, who was right behind him. Finally, after twenty minutes of digging, Steve's flashlight caught a hand moving around. It was John's. Steve grabbed his hand to let him know he was there and then stuck the face piece of his air tank into the crevice near John's hand and gave him fresh air. After more digging, Steve was able to grab John's feet and pull him slightly so that his arms became free. Moments later, an appreciative John Citarella jumped up and gave Steve a big Italian kiss while screaming, "I've never been so glad to see you!" Chief Stack had already run outside to help with the North Tower. It was 10:25 A.M. John and Steve also ran out into the chaos to help. Three minutes later the North Tower collapsed, blowing them to the ground. It was the beginning of a very long day for two old friends, working side by side. John Citarella would never have the chance to say thank you to Chief Larry Stack for helping Steve remove the rubble to help free his body, as the heroic Chief perished in the North Tower collapse. As for John Citarella, he said to his pal Steve, "I'll never make fun of your hands again."

OPPOSITE TOP: In the transfer station, dozens of tools that belonged to the many WTC electricians, engineers, and maintenance workers are stacked up as they are found in the dirt.

OPPOSITE BOTTOM LEFT: On a Sunday evening in January, I was standing just inches from the base of the South Tower Exit Road, also known as the Tully Road, studying the compressed layers of what used to be the first twenty floors and lobby of the World Trade Center. Pieces of torn blue carpeting hung like string from the metal rebar wire, and these papers had been flattened into the mud. They were completed job evaluation questionnaire forms from Dean Witter Reynolds.

OPPOSITE BOTTOM RIGHT: Winter 2002. No matter how clean and warm the men were when they showed up for work at Ground Zero, they would always leave soaked in wet mud with their bones chilled to the core from the high winds that would get sucked into the hole. Charcoal hand- and foot-warmers ("toasty toes") were a valuable commodity.

RIGHT: In the transfer station sits an odd assortment of items representing another period in time, including a PATH train swipe card, a metal subway train passenger handle, a cellular phone, a calculator, a flat Rawlings baseball glove, door knobs, a child's doll, and a business card holder.

PAGES 134–135: Another one of the many odd signs that were unearthed at Ground Zero. We would always do a double take when things like this were unearthed.

PAGE 135: A destroyed van is all that's left in an upper-level parking garage near the PATH train.

133

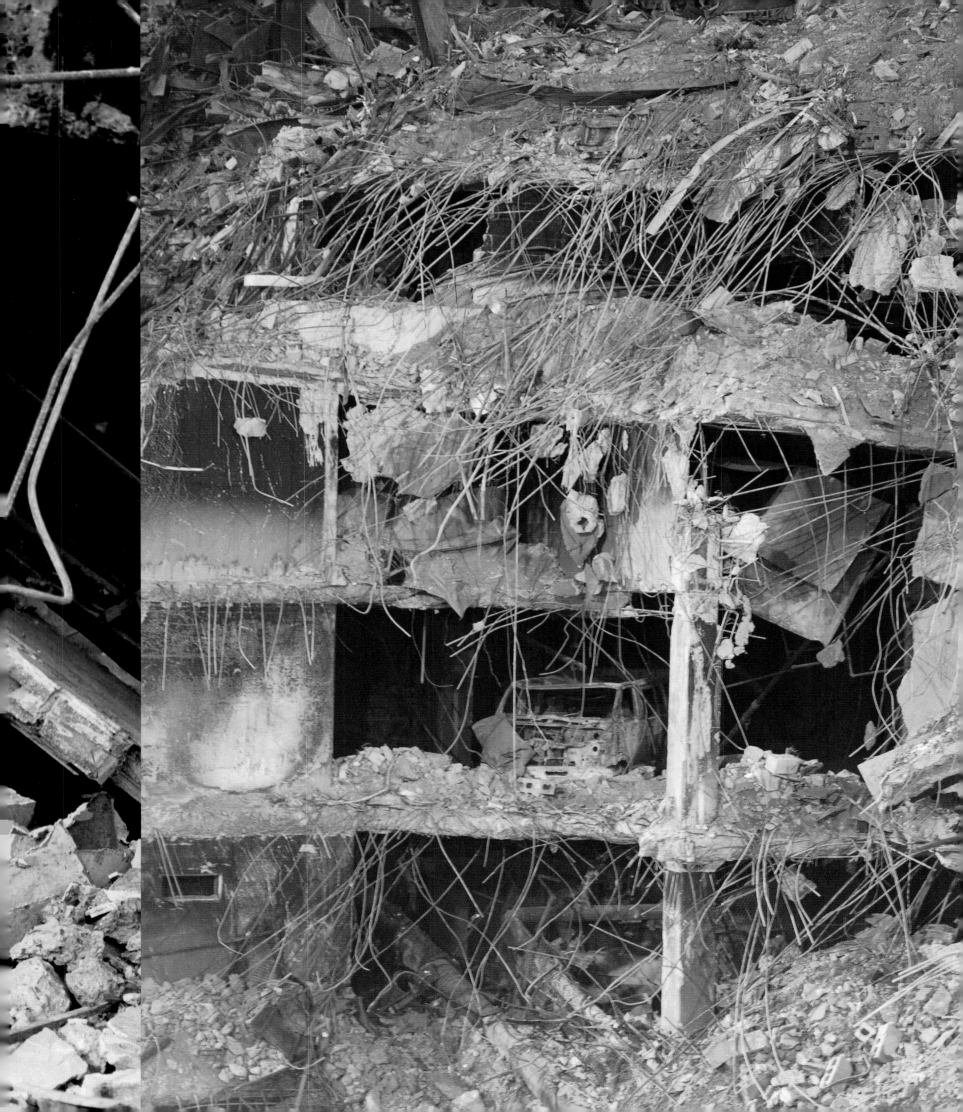

LEFT: It was just hours after the PATH train cars were pulled from the tunnel when I arrived down in the pit. I was taking cover from a thunderstorm under a roof next to what used to be the PATH station when I turned around and noticed this unique perspective of a subway car set against the background of a skyscraper as the rain poured down.

OPPOSITE TOP: An escalator leading from the underground PATH train platforms up to the concourse levels sits out in the open. Yes, it was as creepy in person as it looks here. It led to smoky catacombs that were filled with rubble, concrete, twisted metal, and complete darkness.

OPPOSITE BOTTOM: The view from inside one of the trapped subway cars looking out onto the dark subway platform. A few feet away from this window I found a newspaper dated September 11. It was very eerie on that empty subway car, seventy-five feet (23m) under Ground Zero. The billboard encouraging us to "take advantage" was ironic, since our innocence was taken advantage of in the attacks. But it also reminded me that we need to take advantage of each day and live it to the fullest.

Veteran Firefighter's
Wife and Child
Killed in Bomb Blast

SCHWARZENEGGER

COLLATERAL
DAMAGE

FROM THE DIRECTOR OF THE FUGITIVE

OCTOBER

LEFT: Ironies and symbolism were such the norm for me that by March nothing surprised me anymore. Such was the case when I walked over to the Cortlandt Street 1/9 subway stop, now fully exposed to the air from the collapse, and saw this movie poster, which needs no explanation. The promotional captions above the title only added to the oddity of the find.

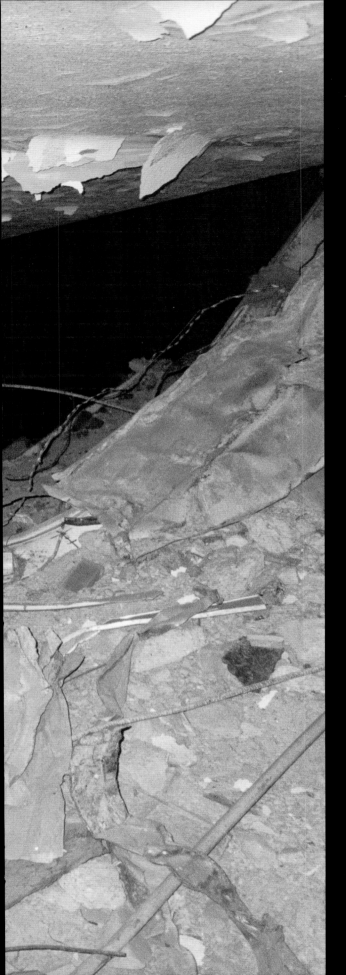

LEFT: The worst type of area to be in at Ground Zero was a confined space such as this one. You are looking at the entrance stairwell for the Cortlandt Street subway stop. It was turned into a landslide of rubble extending all the way to the street. Behind me were the locked turnstiles and gates, so if something unexpectedly collapsed while I was there, I would have had nowhere to run. Needless to say, this was a very short expedition that got my adrenaline flowing. A man's open briefcase sits in the rubble.

ABOVE: Sunrise at Ground Zero, near the destroyed Cortlandt Street subway station.

RIGHT: Chunks of what used to be a beautifully tiled Cortlandt Street subway sign sit at the bottom of the brick wall that had housed the sign for decades.

FDNY CAPTAIN JOHN VIGIANO

There is a photo that appears earlier in this book of a note lying among candles and roses. The note reads, "There are no words to express my sorrow." These were my thoughts when I met an amazing man named John Vigiano, a former Marine and retired FDNY Captain. John's life has been filled with many accomplishments, including winning the battle against throat cancer in the 1980s. But his two greatest accomplishments were his sons, NYPD Detective Joseph Vigiano and FDNY Firefighter John Vigiano II. John's sons were taken from him on the morning of September 11, and the pain that his family and his sons' families have had to endure has tested their strength. Proud does not begin to describe the way John speaks about his sons, as he reflects on the irony of having a fireman and a police officer in the same family. "It certainly added a new dimension to holiday dinners. My sons would often joke about the FDNY and the NYPD. Joe would say the NYPD was best and John, with his great sense of humor, would tease back, saying Joe was correct, since somebody had to direct the traffic while the real men fought the fire." But the respect that each brother had for the other's department was powerful. If Joe, a highly decorated 2nd grade detective and officer in the elite Emergency Service Unit, ever heard someone insult the FDNY, he'd quickly put them in their place. The same held true for John, who would not tolerate anyone making jokes about the NYPD.

"John had visited his brother Joe three times in the hospital over the years when bullets nearly took his life. John knew the seriousness of the job of a police officer." Hearing John speak of his sons, his love could be heard clearly in his voice. "John was like a sponge, soaking up any new techniques he could get so he could be a great fireman. He used to travel around the country with me and teach vehicle extrication [the "jaws of life"] to firemen and police." He was also the biggest Rangers fan there was. Mark Messier was his favorite player and he dreamed of meeting him one day. Joe, who made detective at only age twenty-four, loved his job, and his hard work and bravery earned him the Medal of Honor, the Combat Cross, and three Medals of Valor. Patriotism runs in the family, as evidenced by a moving

story that John shared with me and which is portrayed in the photo that John holds in his hand (below). "About two weeks after my sons died, I went to visit my grandkids, Joe's three boys: Joseph, age nine, Jimmy, age seven, and John, age one. It was my first visit to them since the tragedy and Jimmy knew I was coming, but not what time. I would find out later that Jimmy had stood outside for three hours waiting for me. I arrived to find him standing at attention, dressed in his little Marine fatigues that Grandma had bought him a while back, with his loaded BB gun on his shoulder. Months before, I had given him my old blanket from the Marines, which he had now rolled up into a bed roll and tied across his backpack." As John walked up to him, the first words from his grandson were, "Grandpa, are we ready to go to war?" John, emotional, replied, "No, Jimmy. We have big people doing that for us. You have to stay here and take care of your mommy." John Vigiano spent all his time at Ground Zero during the following months, but never entered the pit area, out of respect for his wife, Jan. "She made me promise never to go in there." Joe had been found but John II was still among the missing. He wanted to go in with the other men and dig, but Jan's words buzzed in his head: "We are all we have together. Without you I have nobody. I need you." And so, John gave his word to Jan that he would stay out of harm's way and maintain his vigil from the edge of the pit. Ironically, in November 2001, while walking around the site, John tripped on some light generator wires and broke his arm. His arm healed rather quickly, as opposed to his heart, which will always grieve for his two sons. Now a full-time grandpa, John gives and receives love from Joe's little boys and John's little girls, Nicolette, age six, and Ariana, age three. John Vigiano makes me feel proud to be an American. In the photo opposite, John proudly displays in his helmet photographs of his two sons, Joe (left) and John II, both of whom perished in the collapse of the Towers. Above, John holds a photograph of his grandson Jimmy dressed in Marine fatigues and ready to fight the terrorists. At top, John embraces the American flag that was used to cover his son Joe for the Honor Guard at Ground Zero.

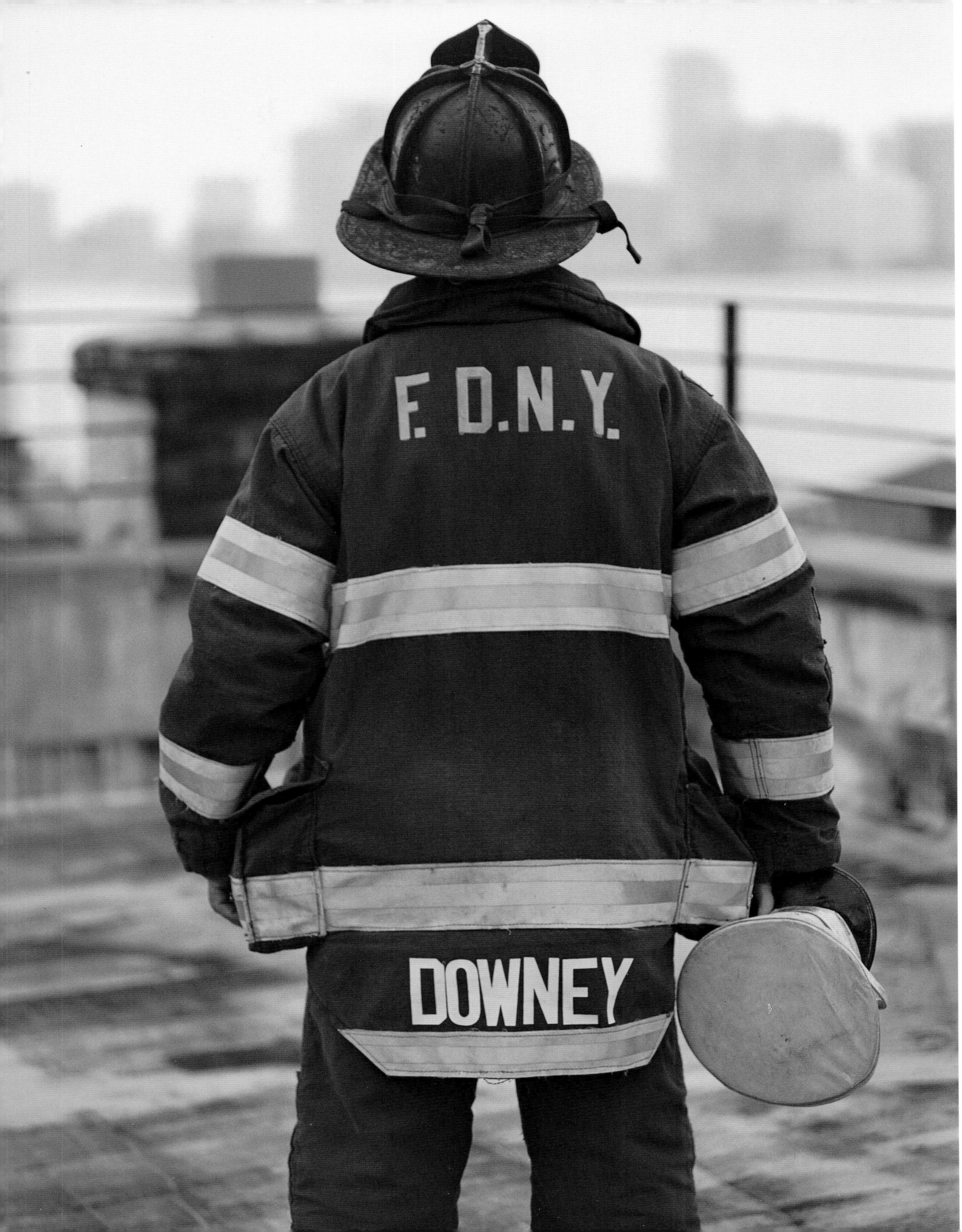
F.D.N.Y.
DOWNEY

ABOVE LEFT: On September 11, when FDNY Captain Joe Downey of Squad 18 arrived at the smoking remains of what used to be the World Trade Center, the first thing he did was approach a fire chief and ask, "Have you seen my dad?" The chief turned away without giving Joe an answer. He could not bear to tell Joe that his father, sixty-three-year-old Deputy Chief of Special Operations Ray Downey, was missing. It was then that Joe knew something was very wrong. Days later, Joe and his two brothers, Ray, Jr., and Chuck, found their father's crushed car and spent hours retrieving personal items, such as one of Ray's favorite caps, which Joe now holds close to his heart. Joe quoted his dad as once saying, "I have no intention of ever retiring. They'll have to throw me out."

ABOVE RIGHT: Joe holds a replica of his father's Deputy Chief helmet. The original was never found.

OPPOSITE: FDNY Captain Joe Downey holds his father's FDNY dress cap, recovered from his father's crushed car at Ground Zero.

LEFT: On a winter day with a high windchill factor, firemen wear masks on their faces to keep warm while digging for victims in the North Tower area. The hole was always colder than ground level, as the winds off the river would get sucked down into the valley. If we didn't dress for the conditions, we wouldn't last an hour.

ABOVE: A fireman pauses while digging to examine what he thinks might be remains.

ABOVE LEFT: Moments before he practically disappeared into a large hole to search for victims, Fireman Bobby Austin of Ladder 111 clears away some rocks.

ABOVE RIGHT: From left to right are firefighters Erik Weiner, Ladder 111, Tim Duffy, Ladder 153, Matt Martin, Ladder 157, Bobby Austin, Ladder 111, Mark Conway, Ladder 113, and Lieutenant Tom Gardner.

LEFT: I was down in the North Tower area when an FDNY bunker jacket was unearthed, igniting a frantic search by the firemen for their missing brother. While the firemen continued a disappointing search that yielded no body, a despondent recovery worker carried the bunker jacket over to a cement block. He laid it down in front of him and gazed out for several minutes onto the massive Ground Zero site, seemingly lost in emotion. When I approached him later and asked what he was thinking about at that moment, he looked down and quietly said, "Can't talk about it."

OPPOSITE: Man and machine search for victims in the North Tower area.

PAGE 150: The claws of a giant grappler pull free a Battalion car that was originally parked on the sidewalk outside the North Tower on the morning of September 11. The car belonged to FDNY Chief Joseph Pfeifer, the first to arrive at the scene.

PAGE 151: The most familiar tools at Ground Zero were mud-covered rakes.

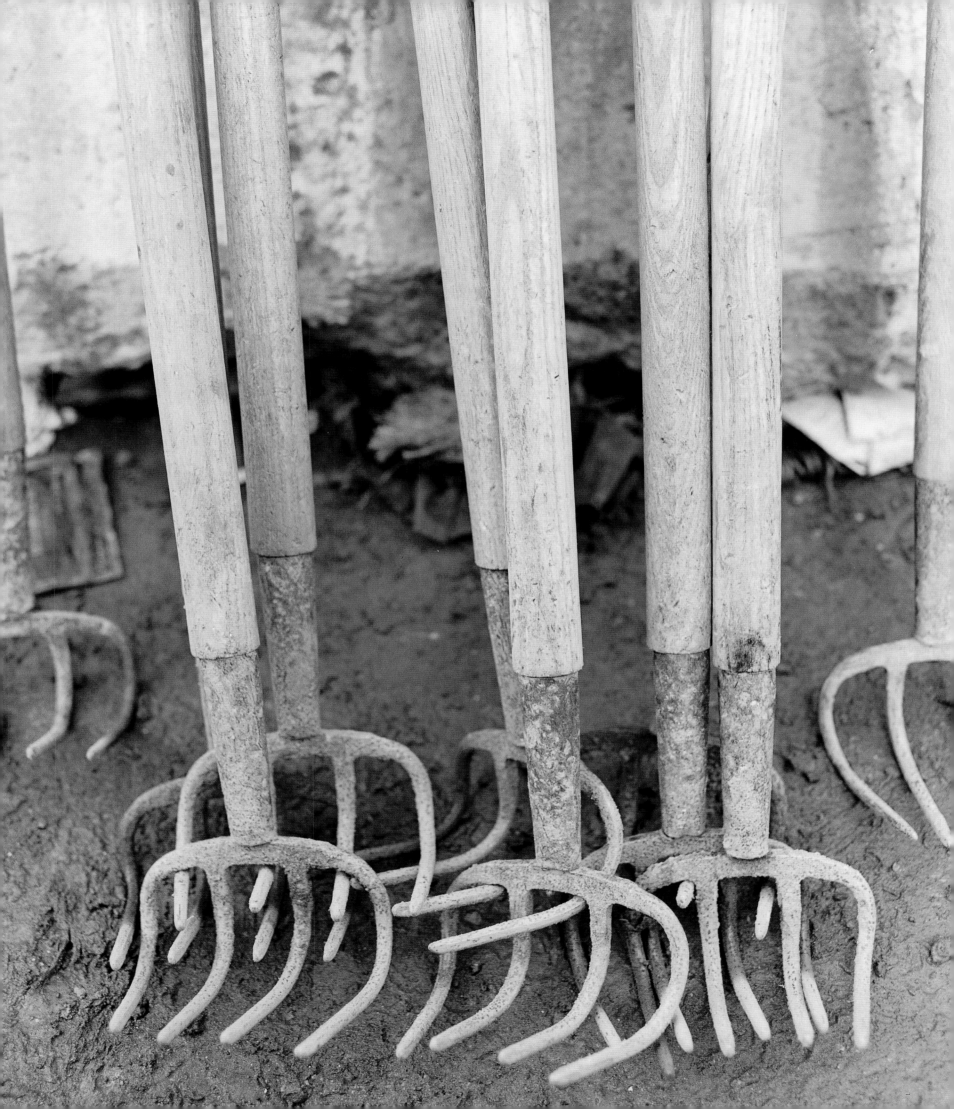

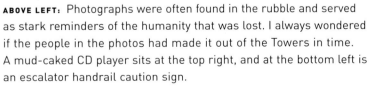

ABOVE LEFT: Photographs were often found in the rubble and served as stark reminders of the humanity that was lost. I always wondered if the people in the photos had made it out of the Towers in time. A mud-caked CD player sits at the top right, and at the bottom left is an escalator handrail caution sign.

ABOVE RIGHT: I was always finding photographs that served as eerie remembrances of an era that was now over. Near where the Secret Service had offices, I found this photo partially buried in dirt and rebar wire. It was taken in 1973 and shows President Richard M. Nixon and someone who is most likely a federal employee conversing at a conference.

OPPOSITE: Transfer station. The first raking of dirt and rubble would take place in the hole. Then, the dirt and rubble would be trucked up to this spot, called the transfer station and located at the top of the pit, where the FDNY and PAPD workers combed through it again, looking for remains. The dirt and rubble were then reloaded onto a truck, sprayed down in the decontamination tent, and carted off to the Staten Island landfill, where off-duty and retired firemen and police officers would comb through it a third time. A very thorough and tedious process, but a very worthwhile one. In this area were found many remnants, which were discarded, and also victim's personal, identifiable belongings, which were saved by PAPD and later viewed by and returned to surviving family members.

LEFT: Dwarfed by a sea of rebar wire, rubble, and dirt, three firemen—looking like children in a sandbox—plan their next spot to dig, with the hopes of recovering a victim. For the most part, there was no science to digging. You just picked a spot and hoped for the best.

ABOVE: An arctic night in January. An ironworker next to me lifts his mask and has a smoke to break the monotony.

LEFT TOP: There was often a private prayer below the bridge if a fallen fireman's company was present. This touching ceremony would happen moments before the final prayer on the exit ramp. Here, the men encircle their fallen brother, removing their helmets out of respect, and listen to the chaplain's words.

LEFT BOTTOM: At the base of the military ramp in the spring of 2002, Deputy Chief Ron Spadafora joins the rest of the firemen in prayer over a fallen fireman. The prayer on the bridge was oftentimes just one of up to three separate prayers that would be said over a victim before he or she left the World Trade Center for the final time. An ambulance waits at the very top to take this fallen hero home.

OPPOSITE: Undoubtedly one of the most moving moments I experienced at Ground Zero is pictured in this image. I was preparing to walk alongside the Honor Guard for two fallen FDNY heroes when I felt a hand grab my shoulder. It was an FDNY Chief, one I had worked with for months and who knew of my photographic work. My initial instinct was that I was in trouble, but it was nothing of the sort. He grabbed my shoulder and literally pulled me into the Honor Guard procession that had begun making its way up the steep hill. I was completely shocked, and upon checking my camera, I saw that I had just one frame left. My heart pounding, I focused on the American flag just feet in front of me as I walked, and wound up capturing what would become one of my favorite images. I then lowered the camera, bowed my head, and slowly marched up the bridge with the men, cherishing the incredible honor that the Chief had given me. Earning the respect of men that I so admired is the greatest honor I could have.

OPPOSITE: Marching through the mud just behind the Honor Guard. We headed toward the military ramp, where almost one hundred Ground Zero workers waited to salute and the chaplain prepared his prayer for the FDNY hero.

RIGHT: "Final Salute." A young firefighter salutes as the men place the body of a hero into the waiting ambulance at the top of the military ramp.

LEFT: The Reverend Mitties DeChamplain was a chaplain at the Ground Zero morgue, and blessed each victim who was recovered during her daily twelve-hour shifts. I first met her one night with a friend of mine, a rescue worker who needed an emotional pick-me-up, the kind that Mitties just seemed to give naturally when we were around her. I cannot say enough about this special woman. She was unassuming, yet had an enormous responsibility at Ground Zero. This photo represents the kind of person she is: a quiet hero who stood in the shadows, performing God's work yet asking for no adulation.

RIGHT: Meet Firefighter Bob Barrett of Ladder 20 in Manhattan. He's holding Twenty, a five-month-old dalmatian puppy given to the firehouse by the sheriff's department of Rochester, New York. Bob retired in July 2002 at age sixty-one. Between fighting the devastating 1975 telephone company fire and losing many of his closest friends in the September 11 tragedy, Bob has seen a lot in his long career with the FDNY.

ABOVE: FDNY Chief William Hines—a very sincere man and one who is easy to talk to—lost forty friends and colleagues in the September 11 tragedy. In the numerous times we spoke down in the hole, his experiences of the September 11 attacks and their aftermath could be seen clearly in his eyes. Like his fellow FDNY heroes, he is simply a sincere man who was on a mission to bring home the missing.

RIGHT TOP: FDNY Lieutenant Terry Nicosia's intense gaze on the last day of his thirty-day tour of duty exemplifies the emotional drain that working in the hole had on everyone. Of the few photos taken of myself in the hole, my friends always say, "Your eyes look different; it doesn't seem like you." It wasn't.

RIGHT BOTTOM: FDNY Chief Robert Turner in the North Tower area in February. One day, I was sitting in the West Hut overlooking the hole, conversing with some chiefs, when I realized I had left a lens down in the hole. Before I could even step foot out the door to race back, Chief Turner, whom I had met for the first time only minutes earlier, offered to drive me down in the gator. His selfless action is a perfect example of the giving nature of firemen, which I always try to convey to people when they ask what it was like working alongside the FDNY.

LEFT: On the six-month anniversary of the attacks, Father Brian Jordan held a prayer service under the WTC Cross. There were no dry eyes as we each took turns calling out the names of people we knew of who had died. I called out the names of firemen Timothy Stackpole and Paul Pansini and NYPD Officer James Leahy, who used to patrol the streets in my neighborhood. There was something very significant about saying a fallen hero's name out loud. It was a powerful acknowledgment of their lives. Moments after the service ended, NYPD officers united in a circle and held hands as their commanding officer read the names of every officer killed on September 11. I climbed on top of a cement barrier to capture the moment on film.

OPPOSITE: To mark the six-month anniversary of the attacks, two large rays of light beam into the sky as a temporary memorial to the fallen. It was nice to see the void in the skyline filled, but it couldn't bring the people who perished back to life. Still, it was a thoughtful gesture that was appreciated by many. This photo was taken from the top of the 10-10 firehouse in Ground Zero, where firemen and police officers gathered to watch the lighting ceremony.

PAGE 164: An engineer makes preparations for drilling into the slurry wall, which separates the Hudson River from the site. When the Towers collapsed, cracks formed, weakening the walls and letting water seep into the site. What you are looking at is called a tieback. Holes are drilled up to a hundred feet (30m) from the top of the wall, cables are inserted, and cement is poured in to keep the wall strong so it won't burst. It was just one of the many projects at Ground Zero that most people were never aware of.

PAGE 165: It was an early morning in March; the sun had just risen. I had been in the hole all night and the previous day, and I decided it was time for some sleep. I turned around to begin my long, muddy walk out of the hole when I saw this fireman, who had been digging for hours, lean back and close his eyes for a moment. This image represents the fatigue, strain, and hopelessness we all felt at times as the hours rolled by with no recoveries.

OPPOSITE: PATH train area, seventy-five feet (23m) below ground level. Exploring the dark tunnels and rooms under Ground Zero with only a flashlight to light the way was like the videos of the underwater exploration of the *Titanic* and made the show *Fear Factor* look like the Disney Channel. This is the controller's room for the PATH train. The sound of dripping water echoed through the room and the floor was slippery with mold. On the desk were newspapers from September 11 and a thermos filled with moldy coffee. This was the wrong place to be if you desire safety. The destruction was unnerving, but when I stumbled upon the calendar that had fallen off the wall and was torn to September 11, my heart skipped a few beats.

LEFT: As I stood inside the PATH train catacombs, the sunrise broke through the twisted rubble and cast shadows on a row of uprooted subway turnstiles. I could not help but think of the thousands of people who passed through these turnstiles for the very last time on the morning of September 11.

ABOVE: Two subway turnstiles stick out of the rubble, and the stairwell underbelly and various concourse levels of the PATH train area sit out in the open, exposed to the daylight. Massive cement slabs, ready to fall at any moment, dangle from skinny pieces of rebar reinforcing rods.

LEFT: While the rear cars of the PATH train were still in the tunnels when the Towers collapsed, the lead cars were not so lucky. They were crushed and compacted into a dirt sidewall, and were unearthed only in January. The passenger seats can be seen inside.

RIGHT TOP: The dirt turns up another eerie sign from the past. This is a cardboard map from the interior of a subway car that showed the World Trade Center as the last stop.

RIGHT BOTTOM: The demolished control room in the PATH train station.

LEFT: Three hundred forty-four. This is the correct number of New York Fire Department personnel who perished on September 11 while trying to save lives. However, the official number has been listed as 343. Meet Arnie Roma, a retired NYPD officer and now a fireman with the Perth Amboy Fire Department. Most importantly, Arnie is the father of a hero, fire personnel casualty number 344. His son, Keith Roma, was a member of Fire Patrol 2. Fire Patrol's duties are to cover furniture and valuables with large tarps and, if necessary, to assist in rescue operations. That's what Keith Roma did on that fateful morning. By eyewitness accounts, Keith had already evacuated three groups of civilians and was in the middle of evacuating a fourth group from the South Tower when it collapsed. Arnie spent months looking for his son with no success. The toughest time was on Christmas Eve, because everyone knew it was Keith's favorite day of the year. Keith loved all the activities that came with December 24, and so on Christmas Eve 2001, Arnie spent the whole day at Ground Zero looking for Keith, but came up empty-handed. Later that evening, Arnie excused himself moments before the Christmas Eve dinner and said he'd be back. His wife, Rosemary, found him in Keith's old room, talking to a photo of his son. She overheard him say, "Don't worry Keith, I'm going to bring you home." Moments later, the phone rang. It was a call from Ground Zero. The man on the other end said there was a positive ID on a young fire patrolman named Keith Roma. He was found next to the nine civilians he was obviously leading out. Keith Roma came home for Christmas Eve.

FDNY CAPTAIN ED SWEENEY

FDNY Captain Ed Sweeney is yet another example of the way a father should love his son. When he speaks of his fallen FDNY son, Brian, he does not hide the pain he feels at having lost him well before his time. After a few minutes of hearing Ed describe his son, and also noticing the uncanny resemblance between the two, I felt as though Brian was there with us. While Brian, a fireman with Rescue 1, was on his way toward the burning Towers, Ed was walking on Jones Beach, enjoying his retirement. When he heard that the World Trade Center had been attacked, he ran back home to find out the latest. After spending the day trying to track his son's location, he came up with no answers. Unknown to Ed at the time, a film crew had taped Brian looking up at the Towers before he made his way into his last fire. Ed had no chance to see his son or to say goodbye. After months of looking for Brian and coming up empty-handed, Ed and his family decided it was best to take some pressure off the situation by having a memorial for him. It was November 26 and Brian's memorial was to take place the next day. Everyone was preparing, and relatives flew in to pay their respects. It was 4:45 P.M. and Ed's relatives had just arrived from the airport when the phone rang. It was Captain Murphy from Engine 288. A fallen fireman from Rescue 1 had been

found at Ground Zero and they thought it might be Brian, but with no dental records, it was hard to make a positive ID. Ed dropped the phone in shock and then composed himself. He thought to himself for a minute; that's when he remembered the eagle. Brian had a large tattoo of an eagle on his back that could identify him. A check was done and it was indeed Brian Sweeney. The memorial turned into a funeral and two days later his son was laid to rest. Here (left, bottom), Ed looks down at a photo of Brian looking up at the inferno in his last moments, before he would attempt to rescue trapped civilians in the South Tower. The inference that his son was looking up at him made Ed emotional; it made me emotional too. I had worked with the fathers at Ground Zero for many months and had engaged in small talk on our breaks, but the portrait shoots made us become closer friends. Before Ed Sweeney left our shoot, he said to me, "The civilians were heroes in their own right for going to work that day. The FDNY went to work also but went above and beyond to help their fellow man and are true patriots."

The artist that created Brian Sweeney's tattoo presented a sketch of it to his father (left, top), Ed, who had a beret added to the eagle and the words, "'Til We Meet Again, Lad."

OPPOSITE: If you ever watched the Chicago Bulls with Michael Jordan and the incredible teamwork they used, then you can come close to understanding the beauty of Squad 41 of Harlem. As these men made a Ground Zero recovery in March, I watched in awe as they worked like a well-oiled machine, knowing each other's moves before they were made. Moments before this photo was taken, three civilians were found. However, a beam needed to be moved to continue the operation. The feet visible at the bottom belong to Gibby Craig, the rock climber—but you can't see him because he's sandwiched under the beam, clearing debris. Ed Walsh, the fireman grimacing with the bar, made his last attempt at moving the beam as I shot this frame. The beam above left was marked "0110," meaning it was from the 110th floor.

ABOVE: We often stumbled upon things in the debris at Ground Zero that left us speechless. It's not like we were pros at how to react; we were no different from anyone else. This was the case when we found the stairwell sign to the 110th floor of the South Tower. We all just took turns holding the sign and nobody said anything. This, to me, was the stairway to heaven sign.

RIGHT: I was near the Cortlandt Street 1/9 subway station when victims were suddenly found and a recovery began. It was considered a successful day— if that's what you can call it—when we could find victims and bring them home. The steel beams near us were marked "0110," indicating that they were from the 110th floor, the top of the South Tower. I saw this fireman scaling a dirt sidewall filled with electrical cables, looking for victims. He wasn't wearing a harness, so I assumed he was either crazy or a rock climber. His name is Gibby Craig, of Squad 41 in Harlem, and he is a rock climber in his spare time. The beam he is leaning on was from the roof of the South Tower.

OPPOSITE: It was a freezing night in February 2002 when I walked down near the base of the South Exit Road for the first time. I had avoided going down there for some time because I knew it would be emotional. For the first six months of the recovery, this road was one of two exits to and from the hole for vehicles and workers (the road is barely visible in the top right corner). It was 4:00 A.M. and I had been photographing rubble for two hours. My hands were frozen and I was getting ready to leave, when I saw FDNY Chief Jack Mooney approach the wall. He stopped in front of a wreath of flowers, which had been placed by a worker on behalf of an FDNY widow, and removed his helmet in prayer. Behind the wreath, a fireman's Scott Pack air tank belt lay in the rubble. The wall of rubble shown here is, essentially, the first thirty-five floors of the South Tower compressed to twenty-five feet (8m). When I wasn't shooting, this is where I would come to pray for the victims, many of whom were still trapped under this road. However, it was so overwhelming that I was often left without words. It was too hard to grasp and I always left filled with anger and the words "Never Forget" ringing in my head. The beam on the far left would later become the last World Trade Center beam to be cut down and transported out of Ground Zero during the final ceremony to close the site on May 30, 2002.

ABOVE: At the request of a mother who lost her son in the South Tower, a Ground Zero worker leaves a flower on the fence that encircles the pit. Technically, no flowers were allowed on the interior fence, but some rules were meant to be broken.

RIGHT: I was at the base of the South Tower road leading out of the hole when I walked up close to the compressed layers of rubble and wire that represented the first twenty floors. Each floor had been reduced to about eleven inches (28cm), and the layers resembled the rings of an old California redwood tree that had been cut down. It was unsettling to see pieces of blue office carpeting hanging down like string from the rebar wire. I was looking at layers of humanity—layers of an era. This was the hardest place in the hole for me to work near. It was graphic and the emotional effects of seeing this area were hard to suppress. It was images like this that often left me without words, especially when people would say "So, what's it like down in there?"

LEFT: Unexpectedly, a void is found in the North Tower area. Firemen lean in with flashlights, looking for victims. Too hazardous for either man or K-9; a grappler moved in to excavate the void.

OPPOSITE: A K-9 pumped with energy is held back by his trainer as FDNY Chief Steve Zaderiko digs where the dog has shown the most activity.

RIGHT: Despite the competition that has always existed between firemen and police officers, many realize that they are all playing on one big team. It was late at night on the South Tower Exit Road when I saw these two workers on a break, engaged in conversation and appearing to have formed a temporary union between New York's Bravest and New York's Finest.

LEFT: Firemen, frozen in their tracks, wait for a K-9 to finish his work. It was important not to move when the dogs were trying to pick up a scent. You didn't want to distract them.

RIGHT TOP: This dog's name is Hansen. He was one of the many search and rescue dogs from the NYPD K-9 Unit, and from units across the country, that served tirelessly at the site, bringing victims home to their families. Hansen was one of the best there was when it came to recovery at Ground Zero. The toughest part about working with him was not being allowed to pet him or give him a big hug when he was working. But we all sneaked in a few hugs here and there.

RIGHT BOTTOM: March 2002. Man's best friend.

ABOVE: Bearing a fallen brother, the Honor Guard heads toward the military ramp, as floodlights reflect off the wet, mud-soaked ground. The stillness of the downtown area at 1:00 A.M. only added to the solemn feel of the moment.

OPPOSITE: The men of Ladder 4, Engine 54, forge through the mud on a spring day to bring one of their brothers home.

BELOW: FDNY Lieutenant Robert Jackson of Engine 54 makes his way up the military bridge on an emotional day in March 2002, when his missing brothers were found.

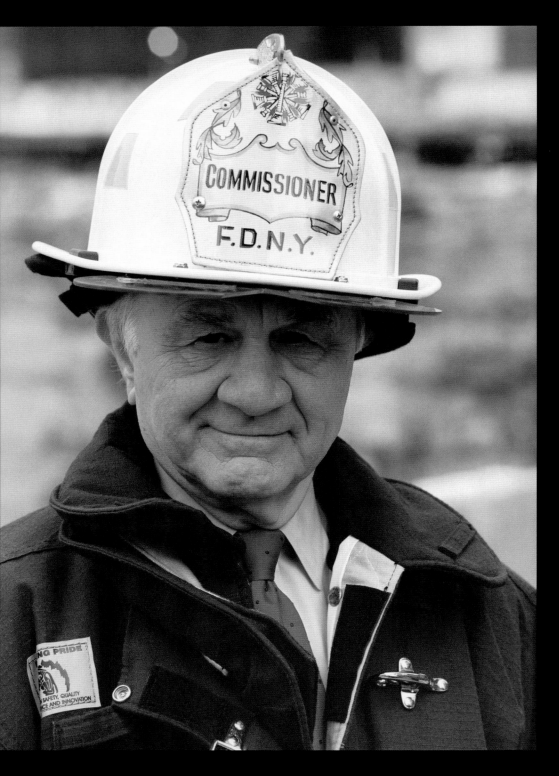

ABOVE: Fire Commissioner Nicholas Scoppetta at Ground Zero in March 2002. On a busy day in the hole for recoveries, the Commissioner had come down to lend emotional support and to assist in the Honor Guard.

RIGHT TOP: FDNY Chief of Department Daniel Nigro.

RIGHT BOTTOM: FDNY Chief of Operations Sal Cassano.

OPPOSITE: Chief Cassano and Chief Nigro stand side by side, running the inner workings of the country's busiest fire department. Nine stars total between the two men signify years of dedication, hard work, experience, and leadership in the Fire Department of New York.

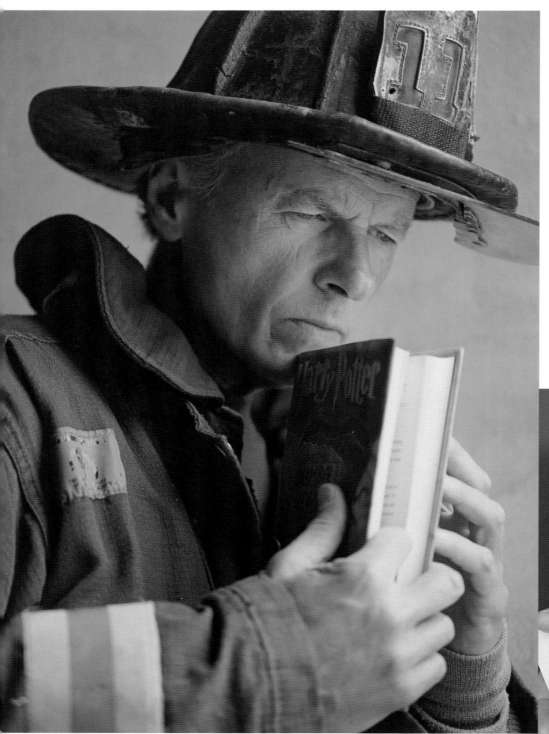

BELOW: Dennis Patrick O'Berg on the day he graduated from the Fire Academy and began his probationary period in the FDNY.

ABOVE: On September 11, Lieutenant Dennis O'Berg was standing in a cloud of ash when he radioed several times for his son, Dennis Patrick O'Berg, but heard nothing back. Lieutenant O'Berg would retire that same day and make Ground Zero and the job of finding his missing son his life's focus. His son, a Probie with Ladder 105, loved reading Harry Potter and was anxiously awaiting the release of the movie. Once, he even shot a self-portrait wearing some Potter glasses as a joke. He was nearly halfway through reading the book when he lost his life—well before his time. Dennis O'Berg took out his son's Harry Potter book when I saw him, and earmarked the exact page his son had left off on before 9/11 changed all of our destinies.

LEFT: George's favorite photograph is the one he took of Kevin as little boy, sitting on the back of his company's fire truck, wearing his helmet, and eating a Popsicle. As much as the terrorist attacks temporarily shook my faith in humanity, the attitude and purity of heart exuded by George Reilly and the other FDNY fathers, brothers, and sons who lost their loved ones has quickly restored it.

RIGHT: Retired FDNY Lieutenant George Reilly is one of the many men I worked with for months in the hole who have touched my life in a positive way. The love that George exudes for his fallen FDNY son Kevin, who was with Ladder 207, is a thing of beauty. There is something to be said for a man who wears his heart on his sleeve, as George does when he discusses the feelings he has for his son, who was his best friend.

OPPOSITE: Late at night, with the Woolworth Building illuminated in the background, rusted pieces of the WTC facade protrude from the rubble.

ABOVE: A woman takes meter readings to test for dangerous levels of Freon vapors. A grappler was digging near an area where Freon tanks were know to have been located, and this precautionary measure was necessary because Freon can kill instantly. Inside the grappler operator's cabs were warning beepers that would go off if the vapors were detected.

ABOVE: In February 2002, I was standing in the rubble of what used to be the North Tower when I was told to put my mask on. While an I-beam covered in chunks of aqua blue powder was moved by a grappler, pieces of this mysterious blue coating fell off into the dirt. It was asbestos.

It was March when we
found the remains of
Engine 55 of Little Italy
about sixty feet (18m)
below sidewalk level in
the north pit. An engine
block (above) was among
the twisted metal, as was
a burnt firehose and the
remains of a six-foot
(2m) hook (right). Items
found in the rubble from
firehouses were usually
returned to the company.

OPPOSITE: March 2002. While everyone salutes, the Honor Guard slowly makes its way up the steep bridge and toward a waiting ambulance.

BELOW: Entering and exiting the hole via the South Exit Road were the activities I most detested at Ground Zero. It was common knowledge that many victims were still trapped underneath and I couldn't wait for the military bridge to be installed and this road to close down. I felt disrespectful to each victim every time I walked on it. I didn't know how to convey these guilt-ridden thoughts, so one muddy day in February, I stood near the base of the road and shot this simple photograph so others could see and feel what I had to experience each day. Guilt, frustration, and anger.

ABOVE: Two FDNY firefighters take a much-needed rest while a grappler moves some rubble. The exhausted men relax on the pile of dirt, gnarled wires, and pipes as if they were lounging on La-Z-Boy recliners. The FDNY—a career focused not on glamour but on the richness of spirit and brotherhood.

ABOVE: At the base of the last WTC beam, memorial posters of
firemen Michael F. Lynch and Gary Geidel were put up along with
others as a tribute before the beam was cut down days before the

LEFT: During the closing ceremony at Ground Zero, bagpipers proudly march up the military bridge, filling the air with their mournful music. Lined up on the bridge, firefighters wearing leis sent over from Hawaii for the final ceremony stand at attention.

OPPOSITE: This was one of the last recoveries made at Ground Zero as we neared the end of a long, nine-month journey. An FDNY firefighter, Stars and Stripes in hand, prepares to make her way down a steep, mud- and wire-filled hill toward a fallen civilian.

RIGHT: In the final Honor Guard at Ground Zero, the men salute as the last WTC beam makes its way up the military bridge on a flatbed truck.

LEFT: The final WTC beam, covered in the American flag and secured on a flatbed truck, rides past me on its way out of the hole. It was very emotional; I realized a major period in all our lives was coming to a close.

LEFT TOP: May 30, 2002. Closing ceremonies. FDNY Deputy Chief Joseph Pfeifer, with the help of EMS Deputy Chief Charles Wells and other uniformed service personnel, places an empty stokes basket containing only an American flag into the waiting ambulance. The flag represented all the victims that were never recovered at Ground Zero.

LEFT BOTTOM: Walking out of the hole with the men as the NYPD shows their support on the side.

OPPOSITE: FDNY Fireman Tim Geraghty, emotional over the loss of his older brother, Chief Ed Geraghty, takes a moment on the last day of the Ground Zero operation to be by himself on the military bridge.

PAGE 198: Everything came full circle for me when the last shot of this project wound up being of Deputy Chief Joe Pfeifer standing on my roof in the exact spot that I was standing on September 11 as I watched the Towers collapse. God bless America and never forget.

IN MEMORIUM
Fallen Uniformed Personnel

NEW YORK CITY FIRE DEPARTMENT
William Feehan,
First Deputy Commissioner
Peter Ganci Jr.,
28th Chief of Department
Ronald Bucca, *Fire Marshal*

Command Center
Gerard Barbara, *Assistant Chief
(Citywide Tour Commander)*
Donald Burns, *Assistant Chief
(Citywide Tour Commander)*

Special Operations Command
Charles Kasper, *Deputy Chief*
Raymond Downey, *Battalion Chief*
John Moran, *Battalion Chief*
John Paolillo, *Battalion Chief*
Lawrence Stack, *Battalion Chief*

Michael Russo, *Lieutenant, Squad 1*
Stephen Siller, *Firefighter, Squad 1*

Robert Hamilton, *Firefighter, Squad 41*

Timothy Higgins, *Lieutenant, Squad 252*

Robert Crawford, *Firefighter,
Safety Battalion*

John Fanning, *Battalion Chief,
Haz-Mat Operations*
Patrick Waters, *Captain, Haz-Mat Co.1*
John Crisci, *Lieutenant, Haz-Mat Co.1*
Dennis Carey, *Firefighter,
Haz-Mat Co.1*
Martin Demeo, *Firefighter,
Haz-Mat Co.1*
Thomas Gardner, *Firefighter,
Haz-Mat Co.1*
Jonathan Hohmann, *Firefighter,
Haz-Mat Co.1*
Dennis Scauso, *Firefighter,
Haz-Mat Co.1*
Kevin Smith, *Firefighter, Haz-Mat Co.1*

Terence Hatton, *Captain, Rescue 1*
Dennis Mojica, *Lieutenant, Rescue 1*
Joseph Angelini, *Firefighter, Rescue 1*
Gary Geidel, *Firefighter, Rescue 1*
William Henry, *Firefighter, Rescue 1*
Kenneth Marino, *Firefighter, Rescue 1*
Michael Montesi, *Firefighter, Rescue 1*
Gerard Nevins, *Firefighter, Rescue 1*
Patrick O'Keefe, *Firefighter, Rescue 1*
Brian Sweeney, *Firefighter, Rescue 1*
David Weiss, *Firefighter, Rescue 1*

Peter Martin, *Lieutenant, Rescue 2*
John Napolitano, *Lieutenant, Rescue 2*
William Lake, *Firefighter, Rescue 2*
Daniel Libretti, *Firefighter, Rescue 2*
Kevin O'Rourke, *Firefighter, Rescue 2*
Lincoln Quappe, *Firefighter, Rescue 2*
Edward Rall, *Firefighter, Rescue 2*

Christopher Blackwell, *Firefighter,
Rescue 3*
Thomas Foley, *Firefighter, Rescue 3*
Thomas Gambino Jr., *Firefighter,
Rescue 3*
Raymond Meisenheimer, *Firefighter,
Rescue 3*
Donald Regan, *Firefighter, Rescue 3*
Gerard Schrang, *Firefighter, Rescue 3*
Joseph Spor, *Firefighter, Rescue 3*

Brian Hickey, *Captain, Rescue 4*
Kevin Dowdell, *Lieutenant, Rescue 4*
Peter Brennan, *Firefighter, Rescue 4*
Terrence Farrell, *Firefighter, Rescue 4*
William Mahoney, *Firefighter, Rescue 4*
Peter Nelson, *Firefighter, Rescue 4*
Durrell Pearsall, *Firefighter, Rescue 4*

Louis Modafferi, *Battalion Chief,
Rescue 5*
Harvey Harrell, *Lieutenant, Rescue 5*
John Bergin, *Firefighter, Rescue 5*
Carl Bini, *Firefighter, Rescue 5*
Michael Fiore, *Firefighter, Rescue 5*
Andre Fletcher, *Firefighter, Rescue 5*
Douglas Miller, *Firefighter, Rescue 5*
Jeffrey Palazzo, *Firefighter, Rescue 5*
Nicholas Rossomando, *Firefighter,
Rescue 5*
Allan Tarasiewicz, *Firefighter, Rescue 5*

James Amato, *Battalion Chief, Squad 1*
Michael Esposito, *Captain, Squad 1*
Edward Datri, *Lieutenant, Squad 1*
Gary Box, *Firefighter, Squad 1*
Thomas Butler, *Firefighter, Squad 1*
Peter Carroll, *Firefighter, Squad 1*
David Fontana, *Firefighter, Squad 1*
Matthew Garvey, *Firefighter, Squad 1*

William McGinn, *Captain, Squad 18*
Andrew Fredericks, *Lieutenant, Squad 18*
Eric Allen, *Firefighter, Squad 18*
David Halderman, *Firefighter, Squad 18*
Timothy Haskell, *Firefighter, Squad 18*
Manuel Mojica, *Firefighter, Squad 18*
Lawrence Virgilio, *Firefighter, Squad 18*

Michael Healey, *Lieutenant, Squad 41*
Thomas Cullen III, *Firefighter, Squad 41*
Michael Lyons, *Firefighter, Squad 41*
Gregory Sikorsky, *Firefighter, Squad 41*
Richard VanHine, *Firefighter, Squad 41*

Patrick Lyons, *Lieutenant, Squad 252*
Tarel Coleman, *Firefighter, Squad 252*
Thomas Kuveikis, *Firefighter, Squad 252*
Peter Langone, *Firefighter, Squad 252*
Kevin Prior, *Firefighter, Squad 252*

Ronnie Gies, *Lieutenant, Squad 288*
Ronald Kerwin, *Lieutenant, Squad 288*
Joseph Hunter, *Firefighter, Squad 288*

Jonathan Ielpi, *Firefighter, Squad 288*
Adam Rand, *Firefighter, Squad 288*
Timothy Welty, *Firefighter, Squad 288*

Joseph Mascali, *Firefighter,
Tactical Support 2*

Fire Patrol 2
Keith Roma

Battalion 1
Joseph Farrelly, *Battalion Chief,
Engine 4*
Calixto Anaya Jr., *Firefighter, Engine 4*
James Riches, *Firefighter, Engine 4*
Thomas Schoales, *Firefighter, Engine 4*
Paul Tegtmeier, *Firefighter, Engine 4*

Paul Beyer, *Firefighter, Engine 6*
Thomas Holohan, *Firefighter, Engine 6*
William Johnston, *Firefighter, Engine 6*

Gregg Atlas, *Lieutenant, Engine 10*
Jeffrey Olsen, *Firefighter, Engine 10*
Paul Pansini, *Firefighter, Engine 10*
Sean Tallon, *Firefighter, Ladder 10*

Joseph Leavey, *Lieutenant, Ladder 15*
Richard Allen, *Firefighter, Ladder 15*
Arthur Barry, *Firefighter, Ladder 15*
Thomas Kelly, *Firefighter, Ladder 15*
Scott Kopytko, *Firefighter, Ladder 15*
Scott Larsen, *Firefighter, Ladder 15*
Douglas Oelschlager, *Firefighter,
Ladder 15*
Eric Olsen, *Firefighter, Ladder 15*

Battalion 2
William McGovern, *Battalion Chief*
Richard Prunty, *Battalion Chief*
Faustino Apostol Jr., *Firefighter,
Battalion 2*

Peter Freund, *Lieutenant, Engine 55*
Robert Lane, *Firefighter, Engine 55*
Christopher Mozzillo, *Firefighter,
Engine 55*
Stephen Russell, *Firefighter, Engine 55*

Vincent Giammona, *Captain, Ladder 5*
Michael Warchola, *Lieutenant, Ladder 5*
Louis Arena, *Firefighter, Ladder 5*
Andrew Brunn, *Firefighter, Ladder 5*
Thomas Hannafin, *Firefighter, Ladder 5*

Paul Keating, *Firefighter, Ladder 5*
John Santore, *Firefighter, Ladder 5*
Gregory Saucedo, *Firefighter, Ladder 5*

Vincent Halloran, *Lieutenant, Ladder 8*

John Fischer, *Captain, Ladder 20*
John Burnside, *Firefighter, Ladder 20*
James Gray, *Firefighter, Ladder 20*
Sean Hanley, *Firefighter, Ladder 20*
David LaForge, *Firefighter, Ladder 20*
Robert Linnane, *Firefighter, Ladder 20*
Robert McMahon, *Firefighter, Ladder 20*

Battalion 4
Matthew Ryan, *Battalion Chief*

Michael Quilty, *Lieutenant, Ladder 11*
Michael Cammarata, *Firefighter,
Ladder 11*
Edward Day, *Firefighter, Ladder 11*
John Heffernan, *Firefighter, Ladder 11*
Richard Kelly Jr., *Firefighter, Ladder 11*
Matthew Rogan, *Firefighter, Ladder 11*

Battalion 6
John Williamson, *Battalion Chief*

Manuel Delvalle, *Lieutenant, Engine 5*

Kevin Pfeifer, *Lieutenant, Engine 33*
Michael Boyle, *Firefighter, Engine 33*
Robert Evans, *Firefighter, Engine 33*
Robert King Jr., *Firefighter, Engine 33*
Keithroy Maynard, *Firefighter, Engine 33*

Patrick Brown, *Captain, Ladder 3*
Kevin Donnelly, *Lieutenant, Ladder 3*
Michael Carroll, *Firefighter, Ladder 3*
James Coyle, *Firefighter, Ladder 3*
Gerard Dewan, *Firefighter, Ladder 3*
Joseph Maloney, *Firefighter, Ladder 3*
John McAvoy, *Firefighter, Ladder 3*
Timothy McSweeney, *Firefighter,
Ladder 3*
Joseph Ogren, *Firefighter, Ladder 3*
Steven Olson, *Firefighter, Ladder 3*

Gerard Baptiste, *Firefighter,
Ladder 9*
John Tierney, *Firefighter, Ladder 9*
Jeffrey Walz, *Firefighter, Ladder 9*

Brian Bilcher, *Firefighter, Squad 1*

Battalion 7
Orio Palmer, *Battalion Chief*

Andrew Desperito, *Lieutenant, Engine 1*
Michael Weinberg, *Firefighter, Engine 1*

Thomas Farino, *Captain, Engine 26*
Dana Hannon, *Firefighter, Engine 26*
Robert Spear Jr., *Firefighter, Engine 26*

Angel Juarbe Jr., *Firefighter, Ladder 12*
Michael Mullan, *Firefighter, Ladder 12*

Gerald Atwood, *Firefighter, Ladder 21*
Michael Fodor, *Lieutenant, Ladder 21*
Gerard Duffy, *Firefighter, Ladder 21*
Keith Glascoe, *Firefighter, Ladder 21*
Joseph Henry, *Firefighter, Ladder 21*
William Krukowski, *Firefighter,
Ladder 21*
Benjamin Suarez, *Firefighter, Ladder 21*

Daniel Brethel, *Captain, Ladder 24*
Stephen Belson, *Firefighter, Ladder 24*

Battalion 8

Thomas DeAngelis, *Battalion Chief*

Robert Parro, *Firefighter, Engine 8*

William Burke Jr., *Captain, Engine 21*

David Arce, *Firefighter, Engine 33*

Thomas McCann, *Firefighter, Engine 65*

Frederick Ill Jr., *Captain, Ladder 2*
Michael Clarke, *Firefighter, Ladder 2*
George DiPasquale, *Firefighter,
    Ladder 2*
Denis Germain, *Firefighter, Ladder 2*
Daniel Harlin, *Firefighter, Ladder 2*
Carl Molinaro, *Firefighter, Ladder 2*
Dennis Mulligan, *Firefighter, Ladder 2*

Jeffrey Giordano, *Firefighter, Ladder 3*

Vernon Richard, *Captain, Ladder 7*
George Cain, *Firefighter, Ladder 7*
Robert Foti, *Firefighter, Ladder 7*
Charles Mendez, *Firefighter, Ladder 7*
Richard Muldowney Jr., *Firefighter,
    Ladder 7*
Vincent Princiotta, *Firefighter, Ladder 7*

Battalion 9
Edward Geraghty, *Deputy Chief*
Dennis Devlin, *Battalion Chief*
Carl Asaro, *Firefighter, Battalion 9*
Alan Feinberg, *Firefighter, Battalion 9*

Robert McPadden, *Firefighter, Engine 23*
James Pappageorge, *Firefighter,
    Engine 23*
Hector Tirado Jr., *Firefighter, Engine 23*
Mark Whitford, *Firefighter, Engine 23*

John Ginley, *Lieutenant, Engine 40*
Kevin Bracken, *Firefighter, Engine 40*
Michael D'Auria, *Firefighter, Engine 40*
Bruce Gary, *Firefighter, Engine 40*
Michael Lynch, *Firefighter, Engine 40*
Steve Mercado, *Firefighter, Engine 40*

Paul Gill, *Firefighter, Engine 54*
Jose Guadalupe, *Firefighter, Engine 54*
Leonard Ragaglia, *Firefighter, Engine 54*
Christopher Santora, *Firefighter,
    Engine 54*

David Wooley, *Captain, Ladder 4*
Michael Lynch, *Lieutenant, Ladder 4*
Daniel O'Callaghan, *Lieutenant,
    Ladder 4*
Joseph Angelini Jr., *Firefighter, Ladder 4*
Michael Brennan, *Firefighter, Ladder 4*
Michael Haub, *Firefighter, Ladder 4*
Samuel Oitice, *Firefighter, Ladder 4*
John Tipping II, *Firefighter, Ladder 4*

Frank Callahan, *Captain, Ladder 35*
James Giberson, *Firefighter, Ladder 35*
Vincent Morello, *Firefighter, Ladder 35*
Michael Otten, *Firefighter, Ladder 35*
Michael Roberts, *Firefighter, Ladder 35*

Battalion 10
Thomas Casoria, *Firefighter, Engine 22*
Michael Elferis, *Firefighter, Engine 22*
Vincent Kane, *Firefighter, Engine 22*
Martin McWilliams, *Firefighter,
    Engine 22*

Walter Hynes, *Captain, Ladder 13*
Thomas Hetzel, *Firefighter, Ladder 13*
Dennis McHugh, *Firefighter, Ladder 13*

Thomas Sabella, *Firefighter, Ladder 13*
Gregory Stajk, *Firefighter, Ladder 13*

Raymond Murphy, *Lieutenant, Ladder 16*
Robert Curatolo, *Firefighter, Ladder 16*

Battalion 11
John Giordano, *Firefighter, Engine 37*

Ruben Correa, *Firefighter, Engine 74*

Matthew Barnes, *Firefighter, Ladder 25*
John Collins, *Firefighter, Ladder 25*
Kenneth Kumpel, *Firefighter, Ladder 25*
Robert Minara, *Firefighter, Ladder 25*
Joseph Rivelli Jr., *Firefighter, Ladder 25*
Paul Ruback, *Firefighter, Ladder 25*

Battalion 12
Joseph Marchbanks Jr., *Deputy Chief*
Fred Scheffold, *Battalion Chief*

Robert Nagel, *Lieutenant, Engine 58*

Battalion 13
Glenn Perry, *Lieutenant, Ladder 25*

Anthony Jovic, *Lieutenant, Ladder 34*

Battalion 15
Charles Garbarini, *Lieutenant, Ladder 61*

Battalion 17
John Marshall, *Firefighter, Ladder 27*

Battalion 21
Robert Cordice, *Firefighter, Squad 1*

Battalion 22
William O'Keefe, *Captain, Engine 154*

Battalion 23
Charles Margiotta, *Lieutenant, Ladder 85*

Battalion 26
Geoffrey Guja, *Lieutenant, Engine 82*

Peter Bielfeld, *Firefighter, Ladder 42*

Battalion 27
Thomas O'Hagan, *Lieutenant, Engine 52*

Battalion 28
Glenn Wilkinson, *Lieutenant, Engine 238*

Battalion 31
Karl Joseph, *Firefighter, Engine 207*
Shawn Powell, *Firefighter, Engine 207*
Kevin Reilly, *Firefighter, Engine 207*

David DeRubbio, *Firefighter, Engine 226*
Brian McAleese, *Firefighter, Engine 226*
Stanley Smagala Jr., *Firefighter,
    Engine 226*

Paul Mitchell, *Lieutenant, Ladder 110*

Battalion 32
Robert Wallace, *Lieutenant, Engine 205*

Ronnie Henderson, *Firefighter,
    Engine 279*
Michael Ragusa, *Firefighter, Engine 279*
Anthony Rodriguez, *Firefighter,
    Engine 279*

Joseph Gullickson, *Lieutenant, Ladder
    101*
Patrick Byrne, *Firefighter, Ladder 101*
Salvatore Calabro, *Firefighter, Ladder 101*
Brian Cannizzaro, *Firefighter, Ladder 101*
Thomas Kennedy, *Firefighter, Ladder 101*
Joseph Maffeo, *Firefighter, Ladder 101*
Terence McShane, *Firefighter,
    Ladder 101*

Martin Egan Jr., *Captain, Ladder 118*
Robert Regan, *Lieutenant, Ladder 118*
Joseph Agnello, *Firefighter, Ladder 118*
Vernon Cherry, *Firefighter, Ladder 118*
Scott Davidson, *Firefighter, Ladder 118*
Leon Smith Jr., *Firefighter, Ladder 118*
Peter Vega, *Firefighter, Ladder 118*

Christian Regenhard, *Firefighter,
    Ladder 131*

Battalion 35
Daniel Suhr, *Firefighter, Engine 216*

Battalion 37
Carl Bedigian, *Lieutenant, Engine 214*
John Florio, *Firefighter, Engine 214*
Michael Roberts, *Firefighter,
    Engine 214*
Kenneth Watson, *Firefighter,
    Engine 214*

Christopher Sullivan, *Lieutenant,
    Ladder 111*

Battalion 38
Thomas Haskell Jr., *Battalion Chief,
    Ladder 132*
Andrew Jordan, *Firefighter, Ladder 132*
Michael Kiefer, *Firefighter, Ladder 132*
Thomas Mingione, *Firefighter,
    Ladder 132*
John Vigiano II, *Firefighter, Ladder 132*
Sergio Villanueva, *Firefighter, Ladder 132*

Battalion 39
Timothy Stackpole, *Captain, Ladder 103*

Battalion 40
Paul Martini, *Lieutenant, Engine 201*
Greg Buck, *Firefighter, Engine 201*
Christopher Pickford, *Firefighter,
    Engine 201*
John Schardt, *Firefighter, Engine 201*

Battalion 41
Stephen Harrell, *Lieutenant, Ladder 157*

Battalion 46
Michael Cawley, *Firefighter, Ladder 136*

Battalion 48
Joseph Grzelak, *Battalion Chief*
Philip Petti, *Lieutenant, Ladder 148*
Michael Bocchino, *Firefighter,
    Battalion 48*

Battalion 49
Carlos Lillo, *Paramedic*

Battalion 51
Raymond York, *Firefighter, Engine 285*

Battalion 57
Dennis Cross, *Battalion Chief*
Ricardo Quinn, *EMS Lieutenant*

Kenneth Phelan, *Lieutenant, Engine 217*
Steven Coakley, *Firefighter, Engine 217*
Neil Leavy, *Firefighter, Engine 217*

John Chipura, *Firefighter, Engine 219*

Brian Ahearn, *Lieutenant, Engine 230*
Frank Bonomo, *Firefighter, Engine 230*
Michael Carlo, *Firefighter, Engine 230*
Jeffrey Stark, *Firefighter, Engine 230*
Eugene Whelan, *Firefighter, Engine 230*
Edward White, *Firefighter, Engine 230*

Steven Bates, *Lieutenant, Engine 235*
Nicholas Chiofalo, *Firefighter,
    Engine 235*

Francis Esposito, *Firefighter, Engine 235*
Lee Fehling, *Firefighter, Engine 235*
Lawrence Veling, *Firefighter, Engine 235*

Vincent Brunton, *Captain, Ladder 105*
Thomas Kelly, *Lieutenant, Ladder 105*
Henry Miller Jr., *Firefighter, Ladder 105*
Dennis O'Berg, *Firefighter, Ladder 105*
Frank Palombo, *Firefighter, Ladder 105*

Battalion 58
Thomas Moody, *Captain, Engine 310*

Chaplain
Mychal Judge, *Chaplain*

**NEW YORK CITY
POLICE DEPARTMENT**
John Coughlin, *Sergeant*
Michael Curtin, *Sergeant*
Rodney Gillis, *Sergeant*
Timothy Roy, *Sergeant*
Claude Richards, *Detective*
Joseph Vigiano, *Detective*
Robert Fazio, *Police Officer*
Ronald Kloepfer, *Police Officer*
Thomas Langone, *Police Officer*
James Leahy, *Police Officer*
Brian McDonnell, *Police Officer*
John Perry, *Police Officer*
Glen Pettit, *Police Officer*
Moira Smith, *Police Officer*
Ramon Suarez, *Police Officer*
Paul Talty, *Police Officer*
Santos Valentin, *Police Officer*
Walter Weaver, *Police Officer*

**PORT AUTHORITY
POLICE DEPARTMENT**
Fred V. Morrone,
    Director of Public Safety
James A. Romito, *Chief*
Anthony P. Infante Jr., *Inspector*
Kathy Mazza, *Captain*
Robert D. Cirri, *Lieutenant*
Robert M. Kaulfers, *Sergeant*
Christopher C. Amoroso, *Police Officer*
Maurice V. Barry, *Police Officer*
Liam Callahan, *Police Officer*
Clinton Davis, *Police Officer*
Donald A. Foreman, *Police Officer*
Gregg J. Froehner, *Police Officer*
Thomas E. Gorman, *Police Officer*
Uhuru G. Houston, *Police Officer*
George G. Howard, *Police Officer*
Stephen Huczko, *Police Officer*
Paul W. Jurgens, *Police Officer*
Paul Laszczynski, *Police Officer*
David P. Lemagne, *Police Officer*
John J. Lennon, *Police Officer*
John D. Levi, *Police Officer*
James F. Lynch, *Police Officer*
Donald J. McIntyre, *Police Officer*
Walter A. McNeil, *Police Officer*
Joseph M. Navas, *Police Officer*
James Nelson, *Police Officer*
Alfonse J. Niedermeyer, *Police Officer*
James W. Parham, *Police Officer*
Dominick A. Pezzulo, *Police Officer*
Bruce A. Reynolds, *Police Officer*
Antonio J. Rodrigues, *Police Officer*
Richard Rodriguez, *Police Officer*
John P. Skala, *Police Officer*
Walwyn W. Stuart, *Police Officer*
Kenneth F. Tietjen, *Police Officer*
Nathaniel Webb, *Police Officer*
Michael T. Wholey, *Police Officer*

GROUND ZERO LINGO

10-10 The defunct Ladder 10, Engine 10, firehouse located fifty yards (46m) from the South Tower and used as the Operations Command Center and tool-supply area during the recovery.

Asbestos Aqua blue fire retardant coating that was used on the beams of the World Trade Center. It is highly dangerous and can lead to serious lung problems if inhaled.

Backhoe Tractor that scooped up and moved dirt.

The bathtub The seventeen-acre (7ha) area where the Towers once stood (aka "the hole," "the pit").

Bovis Main contractor for demolition and removal during the WTC cleanup.

The Bubble "The tent," or the Salvation Army Respite Center. Hot meals were served and makeshift beds were erected here. Open twenty-four hours. Looked like a huge white dome from the exterior.

Bucket brigade The human chain of rescue workers who removed rubble from the hole by passing buckets of debris from man to man in the two weeks after the attacks.

Cab Glass and metal-encased interior of grapplers and trucks where the operators sat and controlled the machine.

Carhartt Brand of insulated pants, jackets, and face masks worn by most FDNY, PAPD, ironworkers, and laborers at Ground Zero during harsh winter weather.

CHS Clean Harbors Services. Ran the cleaning stations that were overseen by the U.S. Coast Guard.

"The church" St. Paul's church, located across the street from the WTC. It was miraculously untouched by the devastation and then used as a rest and relief center, providing physical and spiritual assistance for recovery workers.

Cortlandt Station Refers to the destroyed Cortlandt Street subway station located just outside the World Trade Center.

Crane Used for lifting WTC steel beams.

Cutting station Designated areas at Ground Zero for cutting rebar hanging out of the top of debris-filled trucks. All trucks had to go through the cutting station before leaving the site.

DDC Department of Development and Construction. Oversaw all contractors and construction workers.

Decontamination tent Took dirt and ash off the trucks via workers with jet water hoses.

DEP Department of Environmental Protection. Made sure that there were no environmental hazards at the site.

East Hut Makeshift wooden hutlike command center for the FDNY. Located on the east side of the hole.

EMS Emergency Medical Services.

FDNY Fire Department of New York.

FDNY ATV Unit The jack-of-all-trades of Ground Zero. A team of firefighters that used all-terrain vehicles (called "gators"). Jobs included running recovery tools down to the hole during recovery operations, changing stadium generator lights when the batteries went dead, getting the proper clothing to the men, transporting rubber gloves for the recoveries, bringing the American flags down for the Honor Guard, bringing supplies back and forth, and picking up the heavy, crushed Freon tanks that were found in the dirt. Also exchanged the empty acetylene gas tanks used for welding or any kind of heating. Assisted in recoveries when necessary.

Freon A colorless, odorless, and potentially lethal gas that is heavier than air and displaces oxygen.

Gator Six-wheel-drive vehicle used for quick movement in and out of the pit. Used for rough terrain. Tires blew out constantly from sharp objects in the hole.

GPS Unit Global Positioning Satellite. Used to record the location of individual remains found. The men of the GPS Unit would drive into the hole with the gator to where remains were found and punch the data into the GPS handheld unit, thereby recording the location of every fragment of remains and personal effects. This information was then listed on a master grid and stored in a computer. Operations could then determine which grid areas had the most recoveries and thus help to locate stairwell or elevator shafts, which could mean a higher number of recoveries.

Grappler Machine used to pull up dirt and debris and spread it out for observation.

Ground Zero time A term used when referring to the fact that most Ground Zero workers lost track of the day and time due to the very long hours of work and little to no sleep. Often compared to being in a casino for days on end with no sleep and losing track of the real world due to heavy involvement in the task at hand.

Ground Zeroed out A term used to describe workers who have been in the hole too long and need a break from the unnoticed stress that creeps up on them.

Hallagan A forcible entry tool used by the FDNY. Usually marked with each firehouse's numbers. When a Hallagan was found in the rubble, it signaled that recoveries were most likely imminent.

Hand warmers Small charcoal inserts that became hot for seven hours when exposed to air. Inserted into gloves for warmth during harsh weather.

Handy talky A radio used to communicate throughout the site (aka "the Motorola").

The hole The seventeen-acre (7ha) area where the Towers once stood (aka "the pit," "the bathtub").

Jersey barrier Concrete slabs that ran through the middle of Ground Zero and separated the east side of the pit from the west. The east side was the Jersey side and the west side was the New York side. Term normally used when giving directions to a worker as to where to go to in the hole. Other barriers were also used alongside steep drop-offs at Ground Zero.

K-9s Trained search and rescue dogs. Usually German shepherds but also golden retrievers.

Nino's The restaurant on Canal Street that was open only to rescue workers and fed them for free for many months.

North Exit Road Used to enter and exit the pit in the first four months. Closed down in January 2002.

NYPD New York City Police Department.

OEM Office of Emergency Management. Oversaw the DDC, FDNY, and NYPD.

OSHA Occupational Safety and Health Administration.

OSS Office of Strategic Services. Tested air levels and monitored Freon levels at Ground Zero.

PAPD Port Authority Police Department.

Partner saw Used for cutting concrete. Has a round, twelve-inch (30cm) blade.

PATH Port Authority Trans-Hudson. Refers to the demolished underground subway/train station through which riders were transported between Manhattan and New Jersey. Also had many concourses with clothing stores, newsstands, and bars.

The pile Referred to the sixty-foot- (18m) tall collection of rubble that the WTC had been reduced to. Existed for the first couple of months after the disaster.

The pit The seventeen-acre (7ha) area where the Towers once stood.

Rake Four-pronged tool used to comb through dirt.

Rebar Two-inch (5cm) -thick snakelike reinforcing rods used in construction to strengthen concrete. Very dangerous for trucks to drive over because they can snap back and cause injury.

Rebar cutter Power tool used to quickly cut rebar wire. Used in recoveries.

Sawzall Power tool with six-inch (15cm) blade that cuts through concrete, metal, steel, and iron. Used mostly for recoveries.

Shift change Changing of the personnel at Ground Zero agencies at either 7 A.M. or 7 P.M.

Slurry wall Cement wall surrounding the base of the hole, separating the Hudson River from the site.

South Exit Road Also known as Tully Road. (Named after Tully Construction headquarters located at the top of road. Tully Construction was a subcontractor of Bovis.) Road was used in the first six months of the recovery.

"Spring Street" Nickname for the tool and clothing supply area for firefighters that operated through the goodwill and donations of others. Located on Spring Street.

Stealthlite Lights used on the helmets to free up hands while searching in dark areas.

Stokes basket Metal or plastic stretchers used to carry victims.

Taking a heavy feed Engulfed in heavy smoke.

The tent "The Bubble," or the Salvation Army Respite Center.

Tieback Holes drilled one hundred feet (30m) down, filled with cables, and then filled with concrete. The purpose was to reinforce the slurry wall so it wouldn't burst.

Toasty toes Smaller version of the hand warmer, used for shoes and boots.

Transfer station A designated flat area at Ground Zero where the dirt and rubble would be raked through for the second time before it was taken to the Staten Island landfill for a third raking. The transfer station would change locations periodically but was usually located outside the 10-10 firehouse near the East Hut.

Trenching shovel Compact shovel that can be folded up when not in use. Carried on the waist.

Void A hole or pocket in the dirt or in a structure that's not easily visible to the eye. Can be a good thing that can save your life in a collapse or a highly dangerous pocket to fall into.

West Hut Located on the west side of the hole. Makeshift wooden hutlike command center for the FDNY.

WTC cough Also called the Trade Center cough. A dry, hacking cough experienced by most Ground Zero workers. Most probably caused by the caustic dust, irritants, and smoke in the air.